After fifteen winters, Conan the Barbarian headed south from his home in frozen Cimmeria, fighting to survive in the ancient time known as the Hyborian Age. In his travels, he has gained much, lost much and thrived in bloodshed, as many foes have fallen before

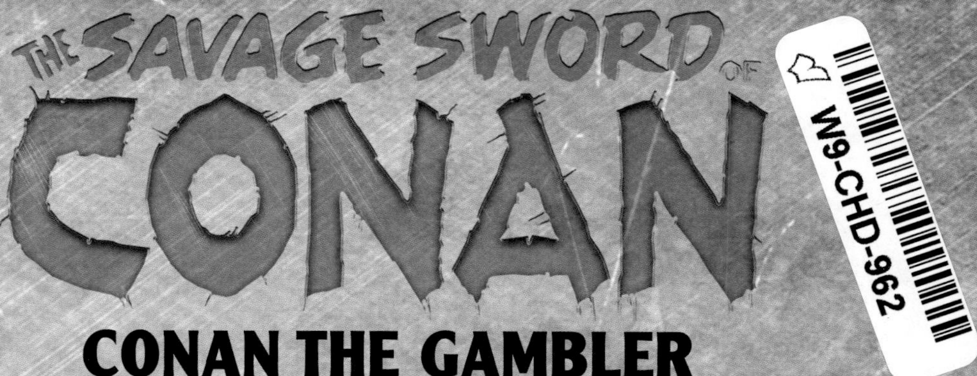

CONAN THE GAMBLER

#6

MEREDITH FINCH ◇ WRITER
LUKE ROSS ◇ ARTIST
NOLAN WOODARD ◇ COLOR ARTIST
DAVID FINCH & FRANK D'ARMATA ◇ COVER ART

#7-9

JIM ZUB ◇ WRITER
PATCH ZIRCHER ◇ ARTIST
JAVA TARTAGLIA ◇ COLOR ARTIST
MARCO CHECCHETTO ◇ COVER ART

#10-11

ROY THOMAS ◇ WRITER
ALAN DAVIS ◇ ARTIST
CAM SMITH ◇ INKER
CHRIS SOTOMAYOR ◇ COLOR ARTIST
MARCO CHECCHETTO ◇ COVER ART

VC's TRAVIS LANHAM ◇ LETTERER
MARTIN BIRO ◇ ASSISTANT EDITOR
MARK BASSO ◇ EDITOR
RALPH MACCHIO ◇ CONSULTING EDITOR

SPECIAL THANKS TO BRIAN OVERTON

FOR CONAN PROPERTIES INTERNATIONAL

FREDRIK MALMBERG ◇ PRESIDENT
JOAKIM ZETTERBERG ◇ EXECUTIVE VICE PRESIDENT
STEVE BOOTH ◇ CHIEF OPERATING OFFICER
MIKE JACOBSEN ◇ COORDINATOR

CONAN CREATED BY ROBERT E. HOWARD

COLLECTION EDITOR JENNIFER GRÜNWALD ◇ ASSISTANT EDITOR CAITLIN O'CONNELL
ASSOCIATE MANAGING EDITOR KATERI WOODY ◇ EDITOR, SPECIAL PROJECTS MARK D. BEAZLEY
VP PRODUCTION & SPECIAL PROJECTS JEFF YOUNGQUIST ◇ BOOK DESIGNER JAY BOWEN WITH ANTHONY GAMBINO

SVP PRINT, SALES & MARKETING DAVID GABRIEL ◇ DIRECTOR, LICENSED PUBLISHING SVEN LARSEN
EDITOR IN CHIEF C.B. CEBULSKI ◇ CHIEF CREATIVE OFFICER JOE QUESADA
PRESIDENT DAN BUCKLEY ◇ EXECUTIVE PRODUCER ALAN FINE

SAVAGE SWORD OF CONAN: CONAN THE GAMBLER. Contains material originally published in magazine form as SAVAGE SWORD OF CONAN (2019) #6-11. First printing 2019. ISBN 978-1-302-91694-7. Published by MARVEL WORLDWIDE, INC., a subsidiary of MARVEL ENTERTAINMENT, LLC. OFFICE OF PUBLICATION: 135 West 50th Street, New York, NY 10020. © 2019 Conan Properties International LLC ("CPI"). CONAN, CONAN THE BARBARIAN, HYBORIA, THE SAVAGE SWORD OF CONAN and related logos, characters, names, and distinctive likenesses thereof are trademarks or registered trademarks of CPI. No similarity between any of the names, characters, persons, and/or institutions in this magazine with those of any living or dead person or institution is intended, and any such similarity which may exist is purely coincidental. Marvel and its logos are TM Marvel Characters, Inc. **Printed in Canada.** DAN BUCKLEY, President, Marvel Entertainment; JOHN NEE, Publisher; JOE QUESADA, Chief Creative Officer; TOM BREVOORT, SVP of Publishing; DAVID BOGART, Associate Publisher & SVP of Talent Affairs; DAVID GABRIEL, VP of Print & Digital Publishing; JEFF YOUNGQUIST, VP of Production & Special Projects; DAN CARR, Executive Director of Publishing Technology; ALEX MORALES, Director of Publishing Operations; DAN EDINGTON, Managing Editor; SUSAN CRESPI, Production Manager; STAN LEE, Chairman Emeritus. For information regarding advertising in Marvel Comics or on Marvel.com, please contact Vit DeBellis, Custom Solutions & Integrated Advertising Manager, at vdebellis@marvel.com. For Marvel subscription inquiries, please call 888-511-5480. **Manufactured between 11/22/2019 and 12/24/2019 by SOLISCO PRINTERS, SCOTT, QC, CANADA.**

10 9 8 7 6 5 4 3 2 1

6 ◇ THE SUITOR'S REVENGE

"Know, oh prince, that between the years when the oceans drank Atlantis and the gleaming cities, and the years of the rise of the Sons of Aryas, there was an age undreamed of, when shining kingdoms lay spread across the world like blue mantles beneath the stars...Hither came Conan, the Cimmerian, black-haired, sullen-eyed, sword in hand, a thief, a reaver, a slayer, with gigantic melancholies and gigantic mirth, to tread the jeweled thrones of the Earth under his sandaled feet."

--The Nemedian Chronicles

Kezankian Pass.
A LANDSCAPE AS FIERCE AND UNFORGIVING AS THE PEOPLE WHO CALL IT HOME.

BUT THERE IS A SON OF CROM WHOSE FIERCENESS IS UNRIVALED EVEN IN THIS HARSH CLIME.
STORM CROW
HIS ADMIRER CONSIDER HIM THE GREATEST WARRIOR WHO EVER LIVED. TO HI ENEMIES, HE IS...A BARBARIAN

HIS NAME?

CONAN.
WHAT DO YOU WANT?

GREETINGS, FRIEND. MIND IF I SHARE YER TABLE?
SUIT YOURSELF.
BLOODY MOUNTAINS! WORSE THAN A WOMAN, I TELL YA. NEVER KNOW WHAT KIND OF RECEPTION YER GONNA GET.

IF THIS IS WHAT PASSES FOR SPRING, IT'S NO WONDER. YA'D **HAVE** TO BE HARD AS NAILS TO LIVE IN THIS, OR EVEN PASS THROUGH.

HERE. FIGURED IF YOU KEN SHARE YER TABLE, I CAN SHARE MY ALE.

BUT, AS YOU SAID...SUIT YERSELF.

ME? I'LL TAKE ALL THE WARMTH I KEN GET. 'S COLD ENOUGH OUT HERE TONIGHT TO FREEZE THE BALLS OFF THE DEVIL HIMSELF.

S THE NIGHT
WEARS ON...
--AN' HE SAYS TO HER, AYE! GRASS DON'T GROW ON A WELL-BEATEN PATH.

HAHAHAHAHAHA! GET IT? 'CAUSE SHE'S A--
HRNGGG...

OME ON. THAT
OKE'S GOT ME
GHS FROM HERE
O CIMMERIA.
HEY! YER
OOKIN' A MITE
CROOKED.
AS WAS THE PLAN.
MAYBE I LOOK FAMILIAR, BARBARIAN?

YOU KILLED MY UNCLE, THORFEL THE FAIR. AND BEFORE YOU DIE, YOU WILL SUFFER... JUST AS I SUFFERED...TEN HUMILIATING YEARS ENSLAVED TO THOSE DIRTY, OUTCAST, HEATHEN PICTS.

I'M GOING TO DESTROY YOUR LEGACY...YOUR REPUTATION...JUST AS YOU DESTROYED MY UNCLE'S.

"AND WHEN YOU FINALLY DIE, EVERYONE WILL KNOW YOU FOR THE SNIVELING COWARD YOU REALLY ARE."
Along the Ilbars River.

A DRUG POTENT ENOUGH TO RENDER THIS WARRIOR OF CROM UNCONSCIOUS DOES NOT COME CHEAPLY. UNABLE TO JOURNEY WITH HIS CAPTIVE, THORGEIR USES THE LAST OF HIS MEAGER FUNDS TO SECURE PASSAGE ON A PASSING TRADE SHIP.
ANOTHER LOAD OF BATTLE FODDER FOR THE GENERAL, THORGEIR?

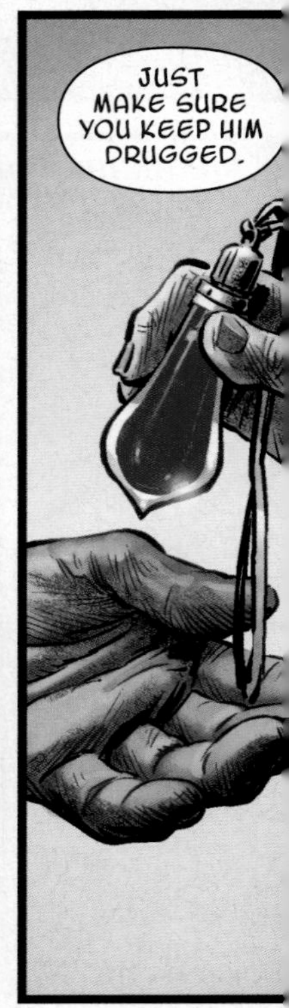
JUST MAKE SURE YOU KEEP HIM DRUGGED.

HAHA! LOOK AT HIM. HOW MUCH TROUBLE CAN ONE MAN BE?

MY UNCLE ASKED THAT SAME QUESTION. IT COST HIM HIS LIFE TO FIND OUT.

THE CAPTAIN KEPT HIS PROMISE, OSING CONAN AGAIN WHEN THEY PULLED NTO PORT IN AKIF.
DRINK UP, BARBARIAN. BY TOMORROW NIGHT, F YOU MAKE IT THAT LONG, YOU'LL BE BEGGING ME FOR THE OBLIVION I FORCE ON YOU NOW.

SLEEP WELL! NOT THAT YOU HAVE A CHOICE. HA!

SPEAK, BEFORE THE RUG WEAKENS ME FURTHER. I WOULD KNOW WHERE I AM.

THE GENERAL OF AKIF SEEKS A SUITABLE HUSBAND FOR HIS PRECIOUS AND ONLY DAUGHTER.

EVERY ABLE-BODIED MAN ON THE CONTINENT IS HERE, FIGHTING TO PROVE IT SHOULD BE HIM.

AND US? WE'RE HERE TO ATONE FOR OUR CRIMES... IN BLOOD.

AS THE LIGHT OF A NEW DAY STREAMS INTO THE HEART OF DESPAIR, A FAINT HOPE RISES UP.

LIFE HAS BEGUN TO RETURN TO THE HEAVILY DRUGGED LIMBS OF OUR CIMMERIAN WARRIOR.

RISE AND SHINE, VERMIN.

TODAY'S THE DAY YOUR MISERABLE LITTLE LIVES ARE FINALLY GONNA MEAN SOMETHING.

I AIN'T GETTIN' PAID TO BE NO NURSEMAID. HOW THE HELL AM I S'PPOSED TO GIVE HIM THIS...

...WHEN HE AIN'T EVEN WOKE UP FROM THE LAST ONE?

SHOVE IT UP HIS ARSE FOR ALL I CARE. HE DON'T NEED TO BE CONSCIOUS. THEY'LL ALL BE DEAD IN THE FIRST TWO MINUTES ANYWAY.

HE CIMMERIAN WILLS HIS INCREASINGLY RESPONSIVE BODY TO STILLNESS, HOPING A GUISE OF UNCONSCIOUSNESS WILL PREVENT ANOTHER DOSE OF THE STRENGTH-SAPPING DRUG.

HIS HOPE IS NOT IN VAIN.

LADIES AND GENTLEMEN, TODAY WE ARE HERE TO WITNESS HISTORY. A FIGHT TO THE DEATH IN WHICH THE STRONGEST WILL CLAIM THE ULTIMATE PRIZE.
LIFE, YES...BUT FAR MORE PRECIOUS: THE HAND OF OUR GENERAL'S DAUGHTER, MAVIA.
MAVIA RODE AT THE HEAD OF AN ARMY ALONGSIDE HER FATHER. SHE HELPED DRIVE OUT THE KESHAN INVADERS FROM THE VERY HEART OF TURAN.

NOW, WITH HER COUNTRY'S INDEPENDENCE SECURED, SHOULD SHE TAKE A CONSORT LESS FORMIDABLE THAN HERSELF IN BATTLE? ***NEVER!***

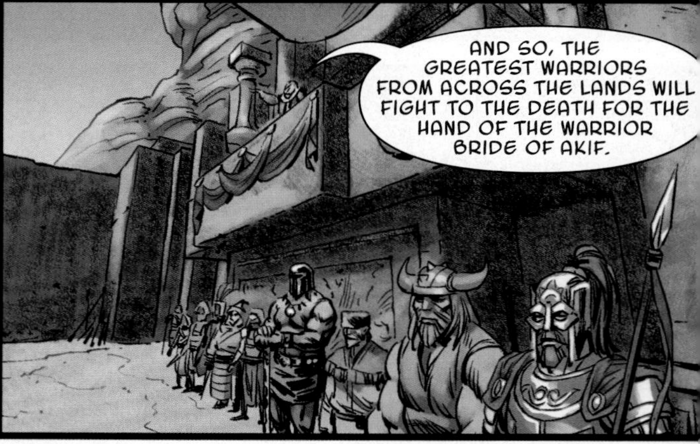
AND SO, THE GREATEST WARRIORS FROM ACROSS THE LANDS WILL FIGHT TO THE DEATH FOR THE HAND OF THE WARRIOR BRIDE OF AKIF.

BUT FIRST, LET US WARM THEIR BLOOD WITH SOME ***LIGHT COMBAT.***

SEND IN THE CONVICTS!

SAVE A SEAT FOR ME IN HELL, FRIEND. BY THE LOOKS OF IT, YOU'LL GET THERE FIRST.

TILL WEAKENED...

...THE BARBARIAN WATCHES DEATH DANCE ACROSS THE SANDS...

SHLUNK
...COMING EVER CLOSER...

..UNTIL IS TURN RRIVES.
HIS BRAIN SLOWLY CLEARING, THE CIMMERIAN WILLS HIS STILL-DRUGGED BODY TO RESPOND BEFORE THE BEHEMOTH'S AXE FALLS.

HE TURNS HIS WEAKNESS INTO AN ADVANTAGE... ALLOWING HIS SLOWLY RESPONDING BODY TO FALL FORWARD...
...STRAINING FOR HIS SWORD, WHILE TH BEHEMOTH, CARRIED BY THE MOMENTU OF HIS MISSED BLOW, RUSHES FORWAR

IT TAKES EVERY OUNCE OF HIS RETURNING STRENGTH TO SLOW HIS OPPONENT...

...BEFORE CONAN RAISES HIS SWORD...

...AND GOES IN FOR THE KILL.
SPLUNCH
YARRGHH!!!

THE FIRES OF ADRENALINE BURN THE LAST VESTIGES OF THE DRUG FROM THE WARRIOR'S VEINS, AND HE KNOWS WHAT NEEDS BE DONE.

THERE IS A BATTLE TO BE WON.

THERE IS VENGEANCE TO BE TAKEN.

AND THERE IS ***NO ONE...***

...WHO CAN PREVAIL AGAINST THIS SON OF CROM.

EN THE MOST
OURAGEOUS
EMBLE BEFORE
E WHO FIGHTS
HIS STEEL-BLUE
N CLOUDED WITH
REDDENED HAZE
A BERSERKER.
AND CRIES
O AJUJO,
BORI,
ARAKHT,
ALI ARE ALL
N VAIN, CUT
ORT BEFORE
EY CAN RISE
UP FROM
BLOODY
NDS TO THE
NHEARING
RS OF THEIR
INTENDED
GODS...
...AS ONE BY
ONE, EACH
CHAMPION FALLS
TO CONAN'S
SWORD, HIS
STRENGTH, HIS
COURAGE...HIS
UNFLAGGING
RAGE.

AND HIS PROWESS DOES NOT GO UNNOTICED.
LOOK AT HIM, SATRAP! HE'S MAGNIFICENT!

BUT... HE...HE'S A CRIMINAL!

HE FIGHTS LIKE ONE **BORN** WITH A SWORD IN HIS HAND. THIS IS NO SIMPLE CRIMINAL. STRONG SONS DEMAND A STRONG FATHER. HE IS THE ONE WHO WILL WIN. ***HE*** IS THE ONE I WILL WED.
BUT HE'S NOT ***IN*** THE COMPETITION.

HE IS NOW!

AS EACH NEW
CHAMPION FALLS...

...THE SATRAP
BECOMES MORE
AND MORE
DESPERATE.

THIS
COMMONER...

...THIS
BARBARIAN
CANNOT BE
ALLOWED TO
PREVAIL.

A TINY SCRATCH IS ENOUGH. THE POISON WILL DO THE REST.
OR WOULD YOU SEE YOUR GENERAL'S DAUGHTER MARRIED TO A FELON?

A TINY SCRATCH... A SIMPLE TASK.

BUT WITH CONAN...

...NOTHING...

...IS...

...SIMPLE.
GRRGLLKKK... GLLLGGGG...!

POISON! THE BARBARIAN HAS BETRAYED US WITH POISON! SEIZE HIM. PROTECT THE GENERAL'S DAUGHTER!

GUARDS RUSH IN TO SEIZE THE VICTORIOUS CIMMERIAN.

STOP! I COMMAND YOU!
BUT THE CONCERN FOR HER UNLIKELY CHAMPION IS UNWARRANTED.

THIS WARRIOR'S PROWESS IS NOT LIMITED TO HIS SWORD.

MY CHAMPION! TELL ME. WHAT IS YOUR NAME?

AND NOTHING WILL PREVENT HIM FROM CLAIMING HIS PRIZE.
I LOOK FORWARD TO SEEING THE PRODUCT OF OUR UNION. OUR CHILDREN WILL BE MAGNIFICENT!

THIS WILL MELT DOWN NICELY.
WAIT! WHAT ARE YOU...?

NO! YOU CAN'T JUST...

...LEAVE.

STORM CROW

A TOAST! TO THE DEATH OF CONAN!
TRULY, MY FRIENDS, REVENGE IS A DISH BEST SERVED C--
TING
TING

End.

#6 VARIANT BY **DAVID FINCH**

7 ◇ CONAN THE GAMBLER PART ONE

"Know, oh prince, that between the years when the oceans drank Atlantis and the gleaming cities, and the years of the rise of the Sons of Aryas, there was an age undreamed of, when shining kingdoms lay spread across the world like blue mantles beneath the stars...Hither came Conan, the Cimmerian, black-haired, sullen-eyed, sword in hand, a thief, a reaver, a slayer, with gigantic melancholies and gigantic mirth, to tread the jeweled thrones of the Earth under his sandaled feet."

--The Nemedian Chronicles

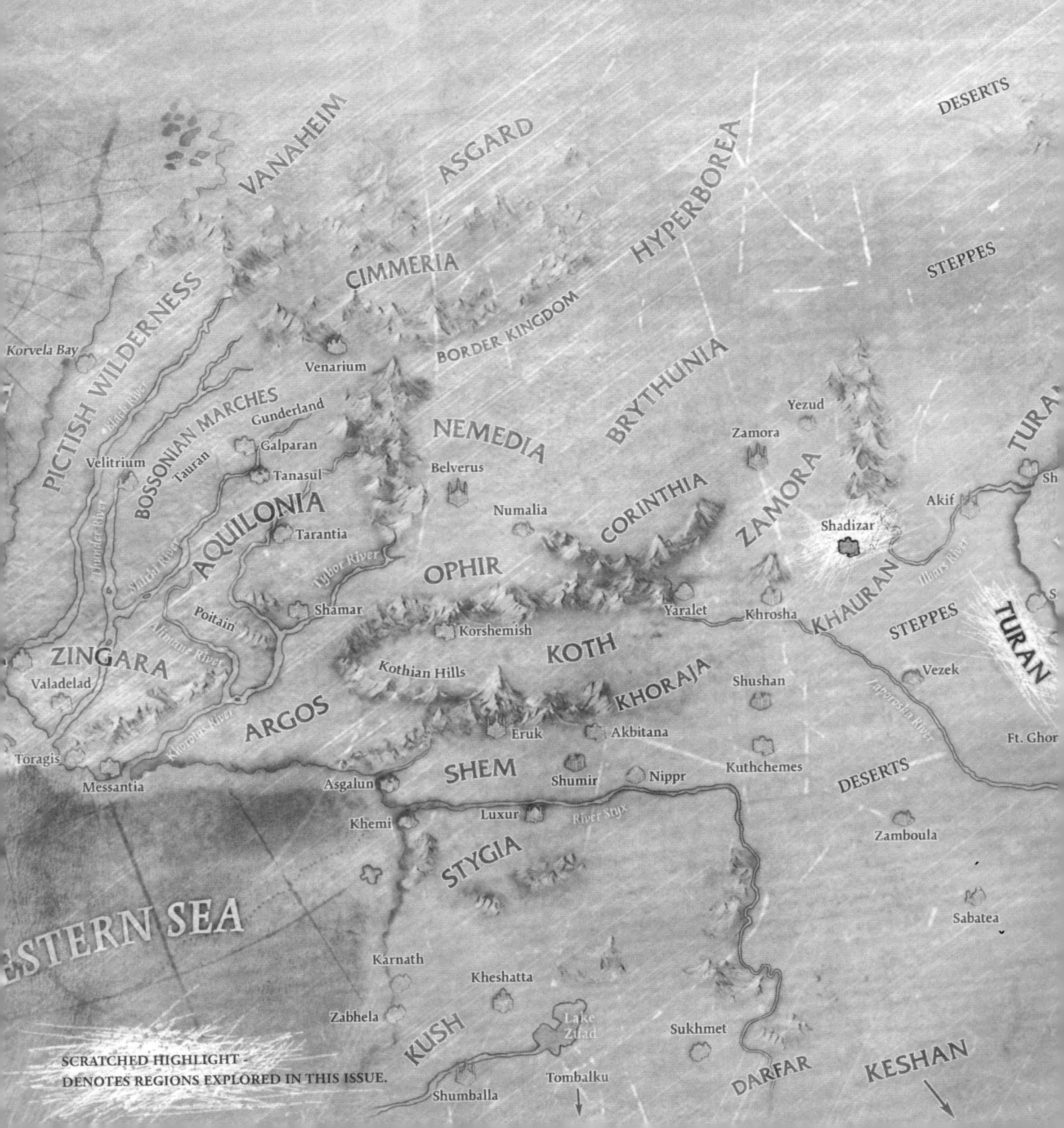

AFTER A DIZZYING TURN OF MEAD AND MERRIMENT IN SHADIZAR THE WICKED, CONAN THE CIMMERIAN INTENDED TO FINISH THIS NIGHT IN GOOD SPIRITS.
THE NIGHT HAD OTHER PLANS.
HELP! HEE-ELP!
WHAT'S THIS, THEN?
CONAN THE GAMBLER

SHUT YER SPEAK-HOLE AND DIE QUICK ALREADY!
HUAAAHH...
OY THERE, DARK HAIR--
TWIST YER GAZE AN' MOVE ON, OR YOU'LL GET ONE IN THE GUT RIGHT NEXT!

YOUNG CONAN WEIGHED HIS OPTIONS.
FOUR AGAINST ONE ODDS FOR A MAN HALF A BREATH AWAY FROM HAVING HIS THROAT SLIT...

S-S-SAVE ME AND I'LL PAY YOUR WEIGHT IN GOLD!

...BUT HE WAS A RICH MAN...

YOU READY TA DIE?

YES...

...BUT NOT BY YOUR HANDS...
...AND NOT TONIGHT!
GUAAAH!

MAKE 'IM BLEED!
YOU CAN TRY...

THESE THUGS TRAINED FOR YEARS IN BAR BRAWLS AND BACK ALLEYS.
THEIR THIRST FOR **MURDER** HAD EARNED THEM RESPECT FROM KILLERS **TWICE** THEIR AGE.
IT DIDN'T MATTER.

THEY LEARNED THE LESSON, AS DID SO MANY OTHERS OVER THE YEARS.

STAY BACK!
I'M GONNA--
PLEASE... DON'T...

A CIMMERIAN WITH **SWORD** IN HAND WILL NOT BE STOPPED IN THIS LIFE OR THE NEXT.

BY THE GODS, THAT WAS GLORIOUS, BOY!
WHO ARE YOU?!
CONAN.

I'M MARAUDUS.
MARAUDUS MAHTIR!
ABOUT THAT GOLD...
...YOU'D BEST HAVE YOUR SCALES HANDY, MERCHANT.

A SWORD ARM AND A SENSE OF HUMOR! I LIKE YOU, CONAN!
WHAT FINE LUCK IT WAS TO HAVE YOU CROSS MY PATH. I'LL NEED MORE OF THAT BEFORE THE NIGHT IS THROUGH.
LISTEN HERE--I'LL DOUBLE THAT WAGE IF YOU ACT AS MY BODYGUARD 'TIL DAWN'S LIGHT.
YOU DO SEEM TO BE LACKING IN PROTECTION, AND MY PURSE IS LIGHTER THAN I'D LIKE...

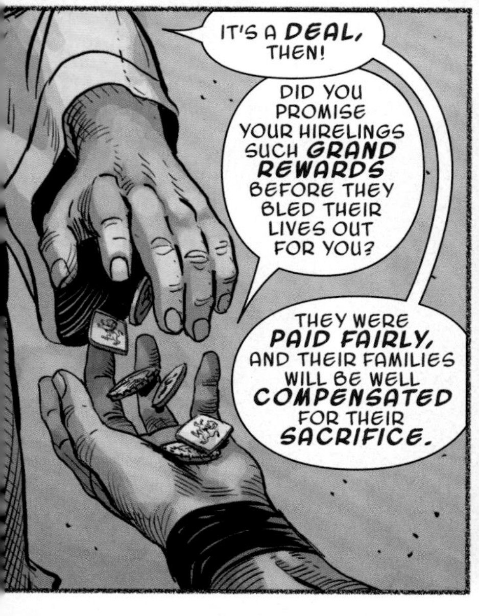
IT'S A DEAL, THEN!
DID YOU PROMISE YOUR HIRELINGS SUCH GRAND REWARDS BEFORE THEY BLED THEIR LIVES OUT FOR YOU?
THEY WERE PAID FAIRLY, AND THEIR FAMILIES WILL BE WELL COMPENSATED FOR THEIR SACRIFICE.

BUT THEY WERE ONLY MERCENARIES...
YOU...
...YOU'RE DEATH INCARNATE.

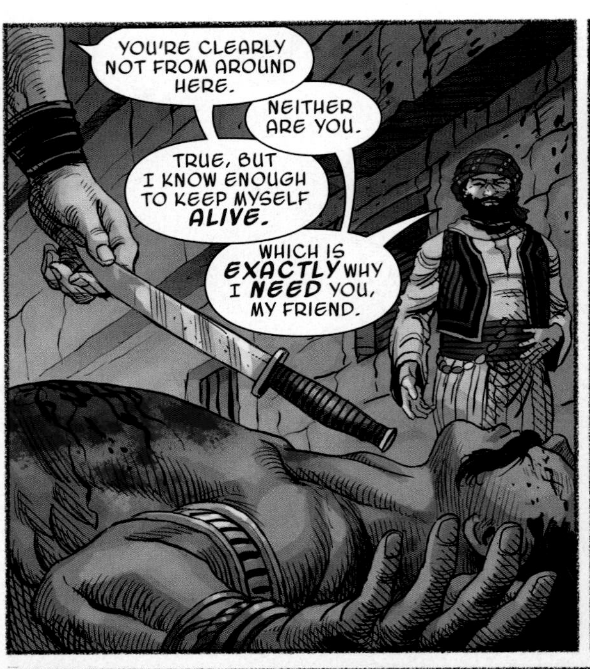

YOU'RE CLEARLY NOT FROM AROUND HERE.
NEITHER ARE YOU.
TRUE, BUT I KNOW ENOUGH TO KEEP MYSELF ALIVE.
WHICH IS EXACTLY WHY I NEED YOU, MY FRIEND.

BELIEVE IT OR NOT, I CAME HERE TO SETTLE A FEUD.
IT SEEMS TO BE GOING POORLY.
NOT AT ALL! THIS SETBACK PUT YOU IN MY PATH.
YOU'RE AS STRONG AS AN OX AND COMPLETELY FEARLESS. THIS IS DESTINY, CONAN.

I DO NOT BELIEVE IN FATE.
THAT'S FINE! I'LL BELIEVE ENOUGH FOR US BOTH.

WHERE ARE WE GOING?
TO A PLACE WHERE ALL DEBTS ARE SETTLED AND KISMET WILL BE OUR COMPANION.

RIDDLES ARE FOR TRICKSTERS AND THIEVES, MARAUDUS. SPEAK PLAINLY.
=SIGH=
IT'S A GAMBLING HALL OF GREAT RENOWN... A PLACE WHERE I CAN END MY DISAGREEMENT WITH A GUILDMASTER NAMED KERO...
KERO THE CALLOUS?
AH, YES, YOU'VE HEARD OF HIM...

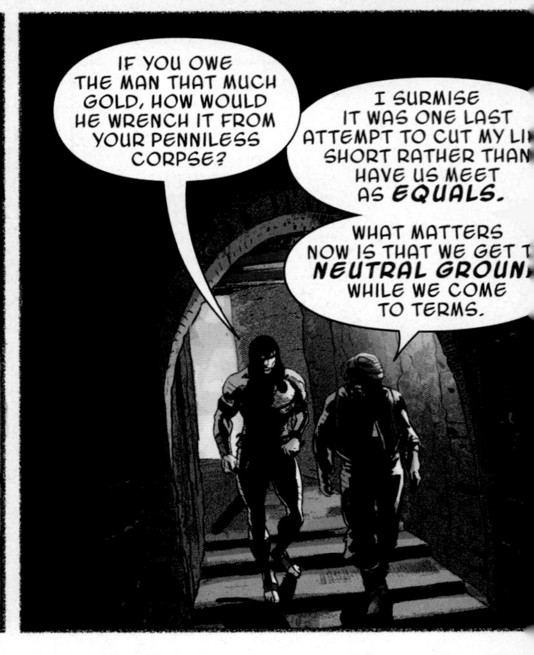

IF YOU OWE THE MAN THAT MUCH GOLD, HOW WOULD HE WRENCH IT FROM YOUR PENNILESS CORPSE?
I SURMISE IT WAS ONE LAST ATTEMPT TO CUT MY LI SHORT RATHER THAN HAVE US MEET AS EQUALS.
WHAT MATTERS NOW IS THAT WE GET T NEUTRAL GROUN WHILE WE COME TO TERMS.

STAY
T MY SIDE
ND FOLLOW
MY LEAD.
GENTLEMEN! WHAT A FINE MOON-TOUCHED EVENING THIS IS!
MARAUDUS... WHAT A SURPRISE.
ARE YOU BACK TO LOSE SOME MORE?
HMPH! THERE'S ONLY WINNING TONIGHT.

YOUR DEBTS TO THE DEN ARE... SUBSTANTIAL.
I'VE PAID DOWN A FORTUNE!
AND YET A FORTUNE STILL REMAINS.
ALL I'M SAYING IS, DON'T LET IT GET ANY WORSE.

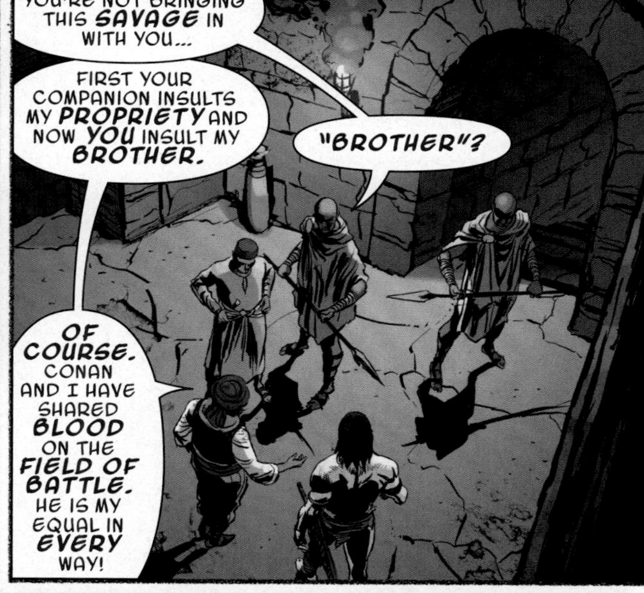
YOU'RE NOT BRINGING THIS SAVAGE IN WITH YOU...
FIRST YOUR COMPANION INSULTS MY PROPRIETY AND NOW YOU INSULT MY BROTHER.
"BROTHER"?
OF COURSE. CONAN AND I HAVE SHARED BLOOD ON THE FIELD OF BATTLE. HE IS MY EQUAL IN EVERY WAY!

IF I AM WELCOME, THEN SO IS HE, FOR WE ARE ONE AND THE SAME! IF YOU WOUND HIM, THEN I SHALL BLEED AS WELL.
IN THE NAME OF MY FATHER, WHO ONCE RAINED GOLD UPON THIS HALL FROM HERE TO MESSANTIA, LET US PASS!

SEE?
EVERYTHING IS FINE.

NOW, MY FRIEND, FEAST YOUR EYES UPON YOUR SURROUNDINGS AND YOU'LL SEE WHY IT'S CALLED--

--THE DEMON'S DEN!

THE BARBARIAN HAD SEEN HIS FAIR SHARE OF ALEHOUSES AND TAVERNS, BUT THIS WAS SOMETHING *ELSE.*

SPICY INCENSE WAFTED THROUGH THE AIR.
LAUGHTER AND BOMBAST PIERCED THE CACOPHONY.

TTERING ANCERS THED TO TRANGE USIC...
...THEIR BODIES A DECORATIVE PATTERN SWAYING ABOVE THE DIN.

AND THREADED THROUGH IT ALL, THE PLAYERS...

...THEIR GAMES...

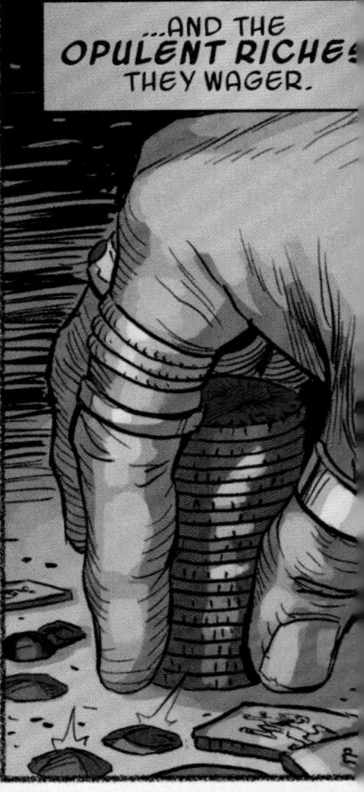
...AND THE OPULENT RICHE
THEY WAGER.

IT'S QUITE A PLACE...QUITE A PLACE INDEED.

WHAT IS THAT?

E CENTERPIECE
F THIS SINFUL
TRONGHOLD.
A "HOLY" ITEM PROCURED BY ONE OF THE OWNERS.
HE CLAIMS IT BRINGS GOOD LUCK TO THOSE WHO PRAY TO IT.

LOCALS CALL IT THE "GODSEND."
HMMM...

I CAN SEE HOW YOUR DEBT PILED UP IN THIS DIZZYING PLACE.
HA! NOT TOO MUCH DEBT, MIND YOU...

.EST I BE FORCED
TO REFUND IT IN
TERTAINMENT."
LET GO! I'LL PAY! I'LL PAY IN PLATINUM!
YOU HAD YOUR CHANCE, SYKES, BUT YOU WASTED IT...

...SO OFF YOU GO TO THE DEBTORS LOUNGE!
NO!

OOOF!
"ENTERTAINMENT"...
PLEASE!
I'LL DO ANYTHING! I'LL--

YARGHH!

CONAN'S EYES WIDENED AS HE HEARD THE MAN'S TORTURED SCREAM ABRUPTLY END WITH THE SNAPPING OF BONE AND TEARING OF FLESH.
THE OTHER PATRONS LAUGHED AND THEN RETURNED TO THEIR GAMES OF CHANCE AS THE MUSIC STARTED ONCE MORE.

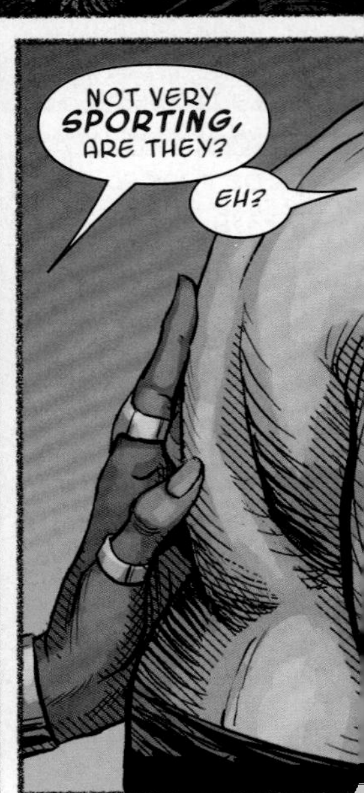
NOT VERY SPORTING, ARE THEY?
EH?

THESE GAMES OF LUCK...
...IT'S SO EASY TO GET LOST IN THEIR ALLURE.

I BET YOU LEAVE NOTHING TO CHANCE...
...IN YOUR LIFE OF STRENGTH AND STEEL.

IF YOU KEEP YOUR WITS ABOUT YOU AND STAY FOCUSED ON THE PRIZE...

...WHO KNOWS WHAT REWARDS MAY BE YOURS FOR THE TAKING?

CONAN!
GET YOUR ASS OVER HERE!

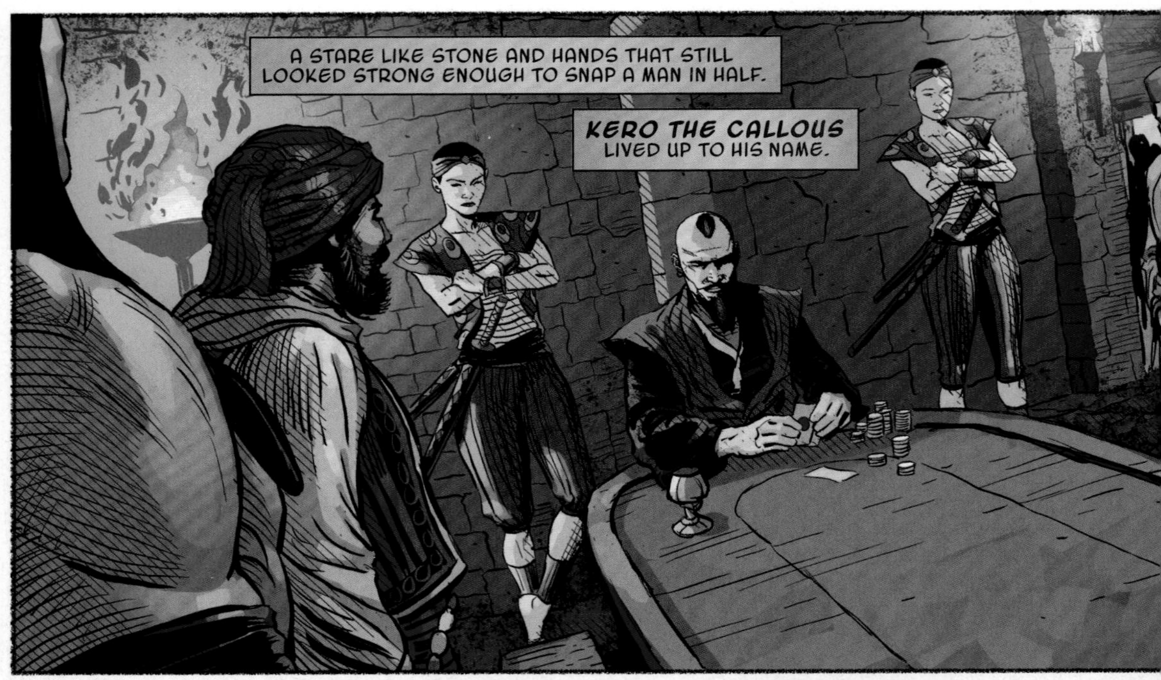
A STARE LIKE STONE AND HANDS THAT STILL LOOKED STRONG ENOUGH TO SNAP A MAN IN HALF.
KERO THE CALLOUS LIVED UP TO HIS NAME.

KERO!
I BET YOU DIDN'T THINK I'D MAKE IT HERE, DID YOU?
NONSENSE. I KNEW YOUR BLOATED EGO WOULDN'T LET YOU STAY AWAY.
SO YOU'RE SAYING YOU DIDN'T SEND ASSASSINS TO SLAY ME TONIGHT?
NOT TONIGHT.

WHO'S THE NORTHERN DOG?

HIS NAME'S CONAN.
HE'S MY BROTHER IN ARMS WHILE I'M HERE.

I'M HERE TO MAKE SURE MARAUDUS IS TREATED FAIRLY.

WE'VE
OTH LOST A
BSTANTIAL
MOUNT OF
SOURCES
HIS COASTAL
ADE WAR
OF OURS...
WHAT WE NEED IS A WAY TO UNRAVEL THE SITUATION WITHOUT SPILLING ANY MORE BLOOD.
EXACTLY!

HERE'S MY SIMPLE PROPOSITION.
WE PLAY A FIVE-GEM OF SERPENT'S BLUFF. THE LOSER TAKES THEIR GOODS AND LEAVES SHEM... PERMANENTLY.
AGREED?

AGREED.

SERPENT'S BLUFF IS A DECEPTIVELY SIMPLE CARD GAME.
EACH PLAYER TRIES TO ASSEMBLE CARDS IN FRONT OF THEM TOTALING AS CLOSE TO THIRTEEN AS POSSIBLE WITHOUT GOING OVER.

T THERE ARE SPECIAL CARDS
HAT ADD COMPLICATIONS.
A SERPENT
CAN "EAT" OTHER
ARDS, ADJUSTING
THE TOTAL.
A KING PROTECTS FROM A SERPENT ATTACK.
A WITCH ALLOWS A PLAYER TO SEE A HIDDEN CARD.
AND ALL SPECIAL CARDS MAY BE PLAYED FACE DOWN AS A BLUFF, BAITING THE OTHER PLAYER TO CALL IT OUT. IF THEY DO AND THEY'RE WRONG, A PENALTY IS PAID.

MARAUDUS HAS EIGHT.
KERO BREAKS.
HA!

BE CALM, MARAUDUS. IT'S ONLY TH FIRST HAND.

YOUR BARBARIAN SPEAKS TRUTH.
SHUT YOUR MOUTH AND LET'S CONTINUE...

I KNOW HOW TO PLAY, OLD BOY.
THOSE TRADE ROUTES WILL BE MINE SOON ENOUGH.

LET ME KNOW IF YOU FANCY PUTTING EXTRA GOLD ON THE LINE...IT WOULD BE NICE TO HAVE YOU FUND MY CELEBRATION ONCE THIS IS ALL OVER.

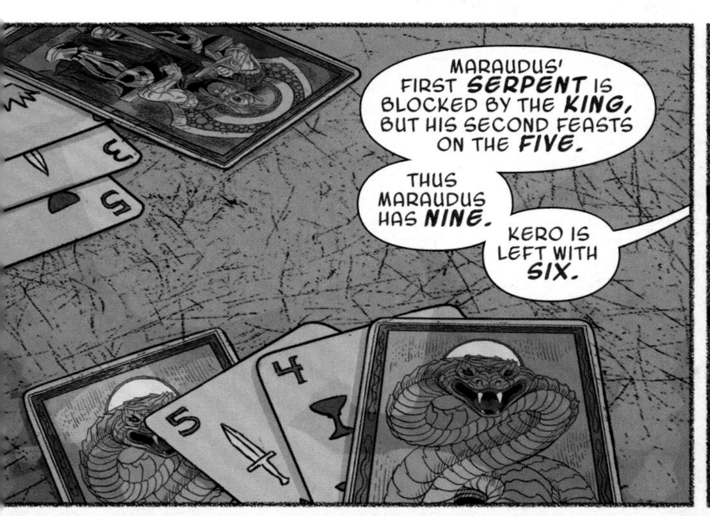
MARAUDUS' FIRST SERPENT IS BLOCKED BY THE KING, BUT HIS SECOND FEASTS ON THE FIVE.
THUS MARAUDUS HAS NINE.
KERO IS LEFT WITH SIX.

CRUSHED HIM THERE!
WHAT FUN!

CONAN KNEW THAT IF IT CAME TO BLOWS, HE COULD SLAY KERO AND HIS ENTOURAGE, BUT DOING SO AND GETTING OUT OF THE DEMON'S DEN WITH HIS HIDE INTACT WAS FAR LESS OF A CERTAINTY...

TOLD YOU!
I TOLD YOU THIS WAS DESTINY!
LUCK MILES UPON US BOTH!

IT'S-- HNNNK--!
MARAUDUS?

THE BOISTEROUS MERCHANT'S FACE FLUSHED RED LIKE **BLOOD**, BUT SOON TURNED **ASHEN**.
HIS BREATH **SPUTTERED**, HIS EYES **BULGED**...
NNGG!

...AND THEN, AS QUICKLY AS IT BEGAN, IT WAS **OVER**.
BY **CROM**!

HE'S **DEAD**.
MAYBE... **POISON**?

YOU SET US UP!
I DIDN'T **KILL** HIM, BOY! THE GAME JUST STARTED, AND I'VE BEEN AT THIS TABLE THE **WHOLE TIME**!

FOUL GAMES AND FOULER **DEEDS**!
THERE'S AN **ASSASSIN** HERE, AND WE HAVE TO **FIND** HIM!
NOT SO **FAST**, NORTHERNER...

YOUR BENEFACTOR, MARAUDUS, PRONOUNCED THAT YOU TWO WERE "ONE AND THE SAME," DID HE NOT?
HE WAS BEING DRAMATIC.
"IF YOU WOUND HIM, THEN I SHALL BLEED AS WELL"...

SAID YOU WERE "BROTHER IN ARMS"...
ODYGUARD.

REGARDLESS... YOU ARE NOW RESPONSIBLE FOR HIS COMMITMENT.
FORFEITURE MEANS YOU GET CAST INTO THE DEBTORS LOUNGE.

EVEN WITH HIS GREAT STRENGTH, THE BARBARIAN KNEW STARTING A BRAWL AT THAT MOMENT WOULD END WITH A BLADE IN HIS GUT AND A SHORT TRIP INTO THE JAWS OF DEATH.

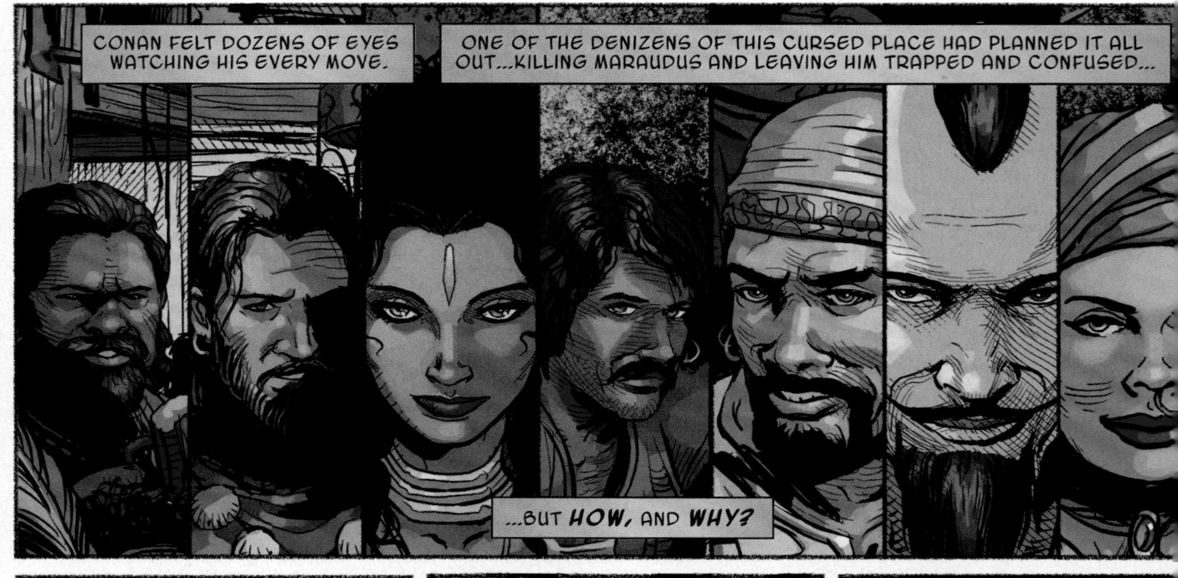
CONAN FELT DOZENS OF EYES WATCHING HIS EVERY MOVE.
ONE OF THE DENIZENS OF THIS CURSED PLACE HAD PLANNED IT ALL OUT...KILLING MARAUDUS AND LEAVING HIM TRAPPED AND CONFUSED...
...BUT HOW, AND WHY?

THERE WAS ONLY ONE WAY TO FIND OUT...

VERY WELL, YOU BASTARDS.

DEAL ME IN.
AND THUS...
...HITHER CAME CONAN THE GAMBLER.

8 ◇ CONAN THE GAMBLER PART TWO

"Know, oh prince, that between the years when the oceans drank Atlantis and the gleaming cities, and the years of the rise of the Sons of Aryas, there was an age undreamed of, when shining kingdoms lay spread across the world like blue mantles beneath the stars...Hither came Conan, the Cimmerian, black-haired, sullen-eyed, sword in hand, a thief, a reaver, a slayer, with gigantic melancholies and gigantic mirth, to tread the jeweled thrones of the Earth under his sandaled feet."

--The Nemedian Chronicles

CONAN NEVER BELIEVED IN FATE.
HE'D SEEN HOW FAITH IN PROVIDENCE BECAME A SHORT TRIP INTO A SHALLOW GRAVE.
GAMES OF CHANCE WERE FOR THOSE TOO WEAK TO EARN THEIR LOT IN LIFE.
AND YET, HERE HE WAS, BENEATH THE STREETS OF SHADIZAR, PLAYING A GAME HE NEVER WANTED IN A PLACE HE SHOULD HAVE AVOIDED.
A CASCADE OF BAD CHOICES.
CONAN
GAMBLER
PART 2
FORTUNE FAVORS THE BOLD

THE CIMMERIAN SAVED A MERCHANT NAMED MARAUDUS MAHTIR FROM A GROUP OF MURDEROUS THIEVES.
CONAN AGREED TO BE HIS BODYGUARD DURING A HIGH-STAKES GAME AT A DANGEROUS GAMBLING HALL CALLED THE DEMON'S DEN.

SIMPLE ENOUGH, 'TIL MARAUDUS DROPPED DE OF APPARENT POISONING THE CIMMERIAN WAS TOLD MUST CARRY ON THE GAME THE MERCHANT'S STEAD

SO NOW CONAN WAS PLAYING A DEAD MAN'S GAME, TRYING TO FIGURE OUT WHO KILLED THE BLOATED BASTARD, AND WHETHER HE WOULD BE NEXT TO JOIN HIM DEAD ON THE FLOOR.

IN SERPENT'S BLUFF, EACH PLAYER DRAWS AND PLAYS CARDS IN FRONT OF THEM THAT ADD UP AS CLOSE AS POSSIBLE TO 13 WITHOUT GOING OVER.
SPECIAL CARDS COMPLICATE THAT SEEMINGLY SIMPLE PROCESS.
A ROUND CONTINUES UNTIL BOTH PLAYERS HAVE PASSED.
2
THE RESULTS OF THE FIRST HANDS DID NOT INSPIRE CONFIDENCE.

KERO'S SERPENT EATS CONAN'S FIVE, LEAVING HIM WITH EIGHT.
KERO HAS TWELVE.

CONAN'S SERPENT IS BLOCKED BY KERO'S KINGS...
...THUS CONAN HAS A TOTAL OF EIGHT AND KERO HAS NINE.

ADMIT IT, NORTHERNER. YOU'RE DROWNING FAST.
YOU DON'T EVEN GRASP HOW TO PLAY, AND I'VE BEEN STACKING THIRTEENS LONGER THAN YOU'VE BEEN ALIVE.
IF YOU FOLD NOW AND BEG MY FORGIVENESS, YOU MIGHT EVEN GET OUT OF HERE WITH YOUR LIFE...

BEFORE CONAN COULD RESPOND TO THE GUILDMASTER'S THREAT, A SOOTHING VOICE CUT THROUGH THE DIN, RAISING THE HAIRS ON THE BACK OF THE BARBARIAN'S NECK.
IT TAKES COURAGE TO REST ONE'S LIFE ON THE FICKLE HAND OF FATE.
THERE IS NO FATE, WENCH.
THERE ARE NO GAMES, EITHER, ONLY CONQUERORS AND THOSE TRODDEN UNDER THEIR FEET...
PRAY TO THE GODSEND FOR GOOD FORTUNE AND MAYBE BOTH OF US SHALL WIN THIS NIGHT.

THE "GODSEND."
A FIST-SIZED EMERALD ENSHRINED IN THE DEMON'S DEN. MANY OF THE PATRONS BESEECH IT FOR LUCK WHEN THEIR CONFIDENCE IS SHAKEN AND DISASTER SEEMS IMMINENT.

CONAN PRAYS TO NO MAN OR GOD BUT, AT ITS MENTION, HIS GAZE DOES LINGER ON THE GLITTERING GEMSTONE.
LIGHT PLAYS ALONG ITS SURFACE AND THROUGH ITS SEEMINGLY ENDLESS FACETS.
THE JAGGED, FLASHING EDGES SEEM TO BREATHE AND DANCE WITH A LIFE OF THEIR OWN.
FOR A MOMENT, THE YOUNG BARBARIAN FORGETS WHAT BROUGHT HIM HERE AND THE TENSION COILED WITHIN HIS BODY.
THE GODSEND'S LIGHT IS WARM AND CALM, AND SO TOO IS EVERYTHING IT TOUCHES...

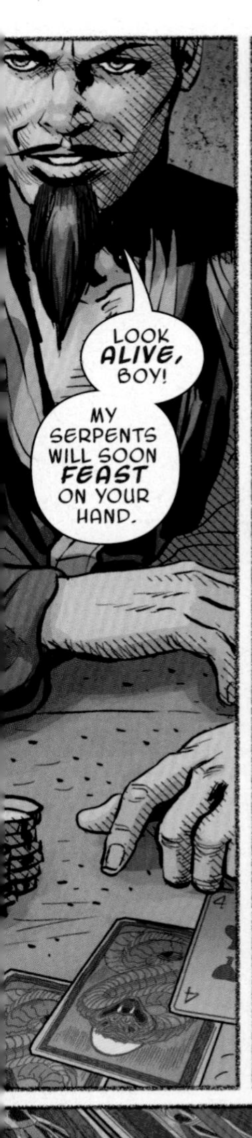
LOOK ALIVE, BOY!
MY SERPENTS WILL SOON FEAST ON YOUR HAND.

I'VE TWO KINGS TO BLOCK THOSE SERPENTS...
...TWO KINGS.

LIKE HELL YOU DO!
I'LL CALL YOUR BLUFF AND TAKE A COIN FOR YOUR STUPIDITY.

ONE COIN FOR ME.

KERO HAS FOUR AND LOSES A COIN FOR THE BAD CALL.
NO CARDS LEFT TO DRAW, CONAN CARRIES WITH SIX.

PLAY ON...

THE BARBARIAN FEELS OUTSIDE HIS OWN SENSES AS THE GREASY CARDS BEGIN TO TURN IN HIS FAVOR.

CONAN'S WITCH REVEALS THE TOP CARD TO CONAN, AND HE SWITCHES IT AGAINST A CARD IN HIS HAND.

CONAN CALLS KERO'S SNAKE BLUFF, ADDING TO THE POT.

NARROW WINS BECOME STAGGERING COMBINATIONS, THE KIND NOT SEEN IN THESE HALLS FOR OVER A CENTURY.

CONAN PLAYS A SERPENT ON HIMSELF TO DISCARD THE FOUR.
A SAVVY MOVE.

CONAN ARRIES TWELVE AND PASSES.

EACH HAND BEATS THE ODDS, AND KERO'S EEMINGLY IMPENETRABLE WALL OF CONFIDENCE BEGINS TO CRACK.

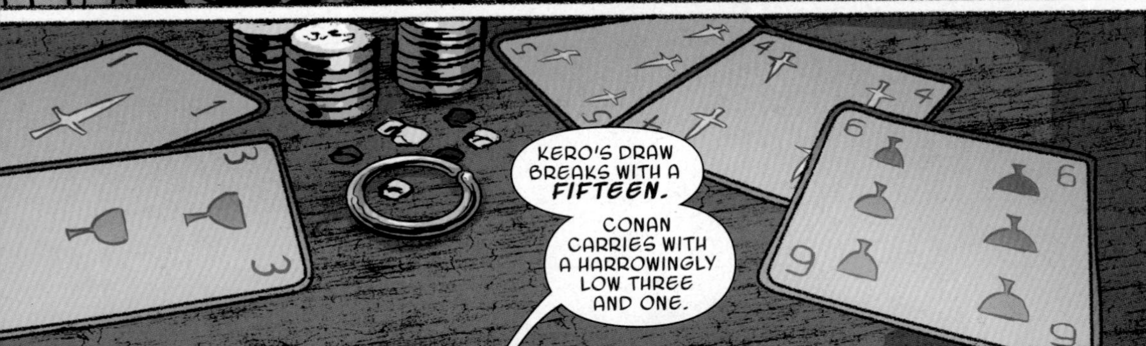
KERO'S DRAW BREAKS WITH A FIFTEEN.
CONAN CARRIES WITH A HARROWINGLY LOW THREE AND ONE.

EACH ROUND SHOCKS THE NORMALLY BOISTEROUS DEN A LITTLE MORE, UNTIL ALL IN ENDANCE ARE STUNNED INTO SILENCE, WAITING WITH BATED BREATH TO SEE WHERE THIS GAME WILL LEAD.

YOUR TRADE WAR WITH MARAUDUS IS OVER AND I'VE TAKEN EVERY JEWEL AND COIN YOU'RE CARRYING FOR GOOD MEASURE.
YOU'VE LOST, KERO.
WALK AWAY.

I'LL NOT GIVE UP TO A DAMN BARBARIAN...

IT SEEMS THE GAME HAS REACHED ITS CONCLUS--
WAIT!

MY FORTUNE.
I'LL WAGER MY FORTUNE FOR ONE MORE HAND, CONAN.
EITHER I TAKE BACK ALL YOU'VE WON AND WALK AWAY VICTORIOUS, OR YOU GET MY MERCHANT COMPANY AND EVERY SCRAP OF GOLD I LAY CLAIM TO.

CONAN WAS ALREADY PREPARED TO LEAVE WITH A TIDY PROFIT FOR HIS TROUBLES, BUT KERO'S RICHES BECKONED BRIGHTLY.
IT WAS TRULY THE OPPORTUNITY OF A LIFETIME.

FORTUNE OR FAILURE, HE HAD TO SEE IT THROUGH TO THE END.
VERY WELL.

EVEN BEFORE THE BARBARIAN GLANCED AT HIS CARDS, HE COULD FEEL THE WARMTH AND CONFIDENCE THAT GUIDED HIS ACTIONS SUDDENLY SLIP AWAY...
...AN EERIE RETURN TO COLD, HARD REALITY.

WHATEVER CAUSED HIS DERANGED RUN OF LUCK, CONAN KNEW ITS TIME HAD PASSED.

THIS WAS ALL A SETUP.

THEY WERE JUST PAWNS IN A GREATER GAME.

THE REALIZATION OF
AT SIMPLE TRUTH WAS
RANGELY COMFORTING
TO THE BARBARIAN...
...AND THUS HE SETTLED IN FOR THE ARRIVAL OF THE INEVITABLE.

DRAW OR PASS?

PASS.

CONAN'S SIX IS EATEN BY A SERPENT, LEAVING HIM WITH **FIVE.**
NO MORE CARDS. KERO CARRIES THE HAND WITH **TWELVE.**

WELL DONE, NORTHERNER.
YOU MIGHT BE THE FINEST PLAYER I'VE EVER SEEN.

A FORTUNE WON AND LOST IN AN **INSTANT...**
...IT SEEMS THESE GAMES ARE NOT FOR ME AFTER ALL.
FAREWELL.

YOU'RE NOT PLANNING ON **LEAVING,** ARE YOU, CONAN?
OUR BUSINESS IS NOT YET **COMPLETE...**

YOUR "BROTHER IN ARMS" CARRIED A CONSIDERABLE DEBT WITH THE DEMON'S DEN.
YOU TOOK MARAUDUS' PLACE AT THE TABLE AND THUS YOU ALSO INHERITED HIS FINANCIAL COMMITMENT TO US...
WE'LL ACCEPT PAYMENT NOW.

YOU BASTARDS!

HOW DO I KNOW YOU AND YOUR CRETINOUS LLIES WEREN'T THE ONES WHO POISONED HIM IN THE FIRST PLACE?

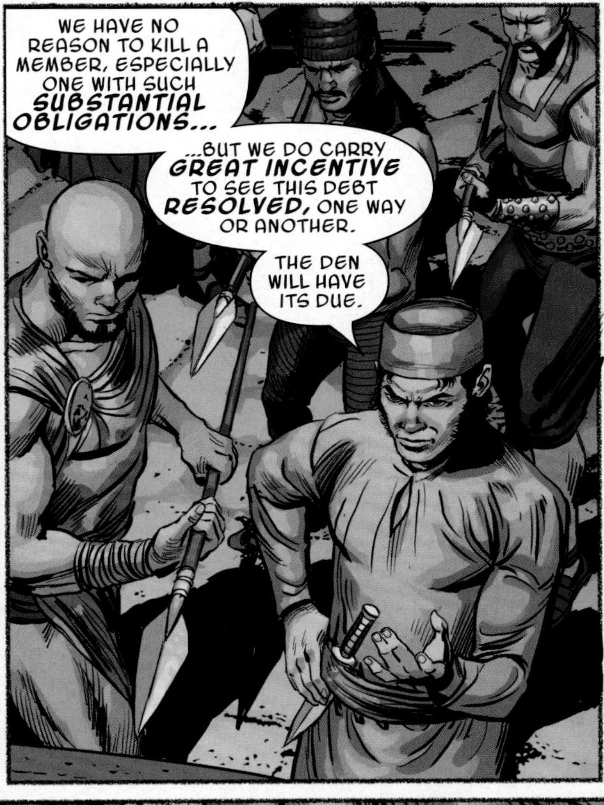
WE HAVE NO REASON TO KILL A MEMBER, ESPECIALLY ONE WITH SUCH SUBSTANTIAL OBLIGATIONS...
...BUT WE DO CARRY GREAT INCENTIVE TO SEE THIS DEBT RESOLVED, ONE WAY OR ANOTHER.
THE DEN WILL HAVE ITS DUE.

AND THERE, THE BARBARIAN REALIZED THE TRUE DEPTH OF HIS FOOLISHNESS...

...HE LET HIMSELF BE PLAYED AND THEN THOUGHT HE COULD WALK AWAY UNSCATHED.

NO MORE RULES OR RECEIPTS.
NO MORE CARDS OR COINS.
THE TIME FOR GAMES WAS OVER.

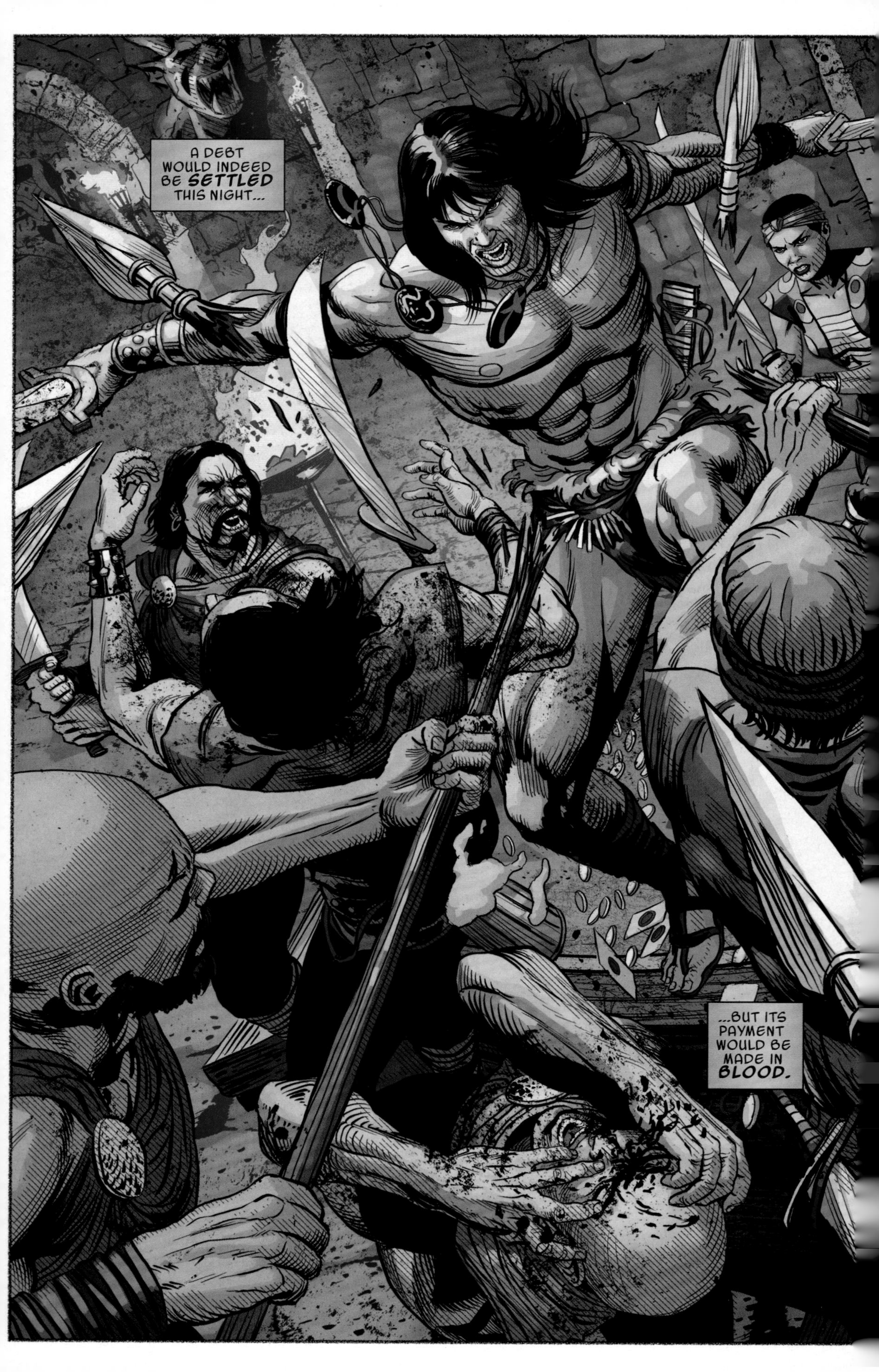
A DEBT WOULD INDEED BE SETTLED THIS NIGHT...
...BUT ITS PAYMENT WOULD BE MADE IN BLOOD.

THE BLOOD OF GUARDSMEN, FOLLOWING ORDERS NO MATTER HOW TWISTED.

THE BLOOD OF MERCENARIES, EAGER TO PROVE THEIR WORTH TO THEIR SNIVELING MASTERS.

THE BLOOD OF THE RICH, BUILT ON A LIFETIME OF TRICKS AND TREACHERY.

ANY BLOOD WOULD DO...
...JUST SO LONG AS IT DRIPPED FROM CONAN'S BLADE.

ONE MAN AGAINST TWO DOZEN HARDLY SEEMS FAIR.

BUT WHEN THAT ONE IS CIMMERIAN-BORN...

...FORGED WITH SINEW AND STEEL...

...THE ODDS ARE FAR LESS CERTAIN.
IF THIS WERE A BATTLEFIELD, CONAN WOULD BE ABLE TO WATCH HIS FLANKS AND KEEP HIS FOES AT A DISTANCE.

HERE, IN SUCH CLOSE QUARTERS WITH SO MANY OPPONENTS, THE BARBARIAN IS PRESSED FROM ALL SIDES DESPITE HIS BEST EFFORTS.
ONE MISTAKE, AND THE ADVANTAGE HIS FURY GAINED HIM IS LOST...
ONE MISTAKE...
...AND THERE IS NO ESCAPE.

YOU'RE A SAVAGE ONE, AREN'T YOU?
WELL, WE HAVE JUST THE THING FOR THAT.

TOSS THE ANIMAL WHERE HE BELONGS...

...INTO THE DEBTORS LOUNGE!

HERE'S YOUR WEAPON, DOG.
IT WON'T SAVE YOU FROM THE BRUTE, BUT IT'LL AMUSE US TO WATCH YOU TRY.

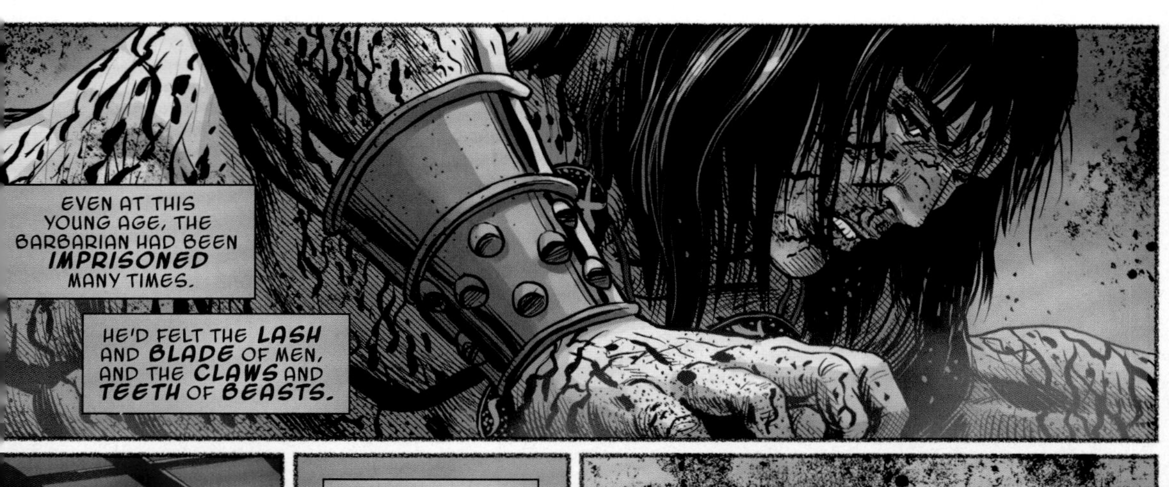
EVEN AT THIS YOUNG AGE, THE BARBARIAN HAD BEEN IMPRISONED MANY TIMES.
HE'D FELT THE LASH AND BLADE OF MEN, AND THE CLAWS AND TEETH OF BEASTS.

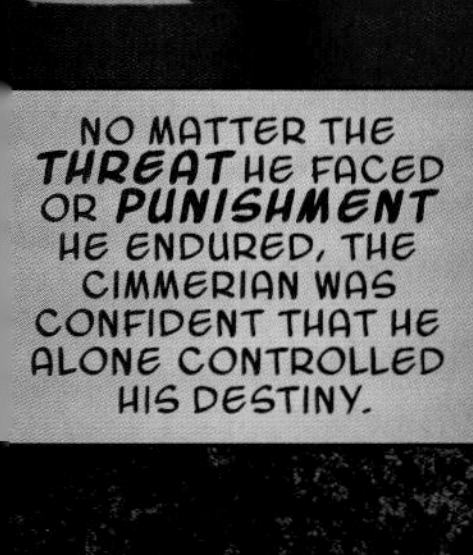
NO MATTER THE THREAT HE FACED OR PUNISHMENT HE ENDURED, THE CIMMERIAN WAS CONFIDENT THAT HE ALONE CONTROLLED HIS DESTINY.

BUT THERE, IN A PIT OF HORROR BENEATH THE STREETS OF SHADIZAR, AS WEALTHY FIENDS JEERED AT HIM FROM ABOVE...

...CONAN FINALLY WONDERED IF FATE HAD INDEED BROUGHT HIM TO THIS PLACE...

...AS HE GLIMPSED HIS LIFE'S END REFLECTED IN THE BLAZING EYES OF A CREATURE MOST FOUL.

9 ◇ CONAN THE GAMBLER PART THREE

"Know, oh prince, that between the years when the oceans drank Atlantis and the gleaming cities, and the years of the rise of the Sons of Aryas, there was an age undreamed of, when shining kingdoms lay spread across the world like blue mantles beneath the stars...Hither came Conan, the Cimmerian, black-haired, sullen-eyed, sword in hand, a thief, a reaver, a slayer, with gigantic melancholies and gigantic mirth, to tread the jeweled thrones of the Earth under his sandaled feet."

--The Nemedian Chronicles

"THE DEBTORS LOUNGE."
A BANAL NAME FOR A DEADLY PLACE WHERE MEMBERS OF THE DEMON'S DEN ARE CAST WHEN THEY CANNOT HONOR THEIR COMMITMENTS.
THE LATEST OCCUPANT OF THIS PIT OF PAIN?
CONAN THE GAMBLER.

THE MONSTROUS DENIZEN WHO RESIDES HERE BREAKS BONES AND FEASTS ON FLESH.
IF THERE IS A LIMIT TO ITS HUNGER, THE GUARDS AND PATRONS OF THE DEN HAVE YET TO FIND IT.
COME THEN, FILTHY BEAST!
THE BASTARDS OVER OUR HEADS EXPECT A GOOD SHOW, SO LET'S GIVE THEM ONE THEY'LL NEVER FORGET!

ABOVE CONAN RANG CHEERS AND BELLOWS FROM A BLOODTHIRSTY CROWD OF GAMBLERS AND GUARDSMEN.

BENEATH THE BARBARIAN'S FEET, WET SAND AND THE ROTTING REMAINS OF THE LOUNGE'S PREVIOUS "VISITORS."

BUT, WITH BLADE IN HAND AND BLOOD COURSING THROUGH HIS VEINS, THE CIMMERIAN COULD FINALLY FOCUS HIS VIOLENT NEEDS ON A TARGET WORTHY OF HIS ANGER.

STEEL VERSUS STONY FLESH.
FURY VERSUS CRUSHING MIGHT.

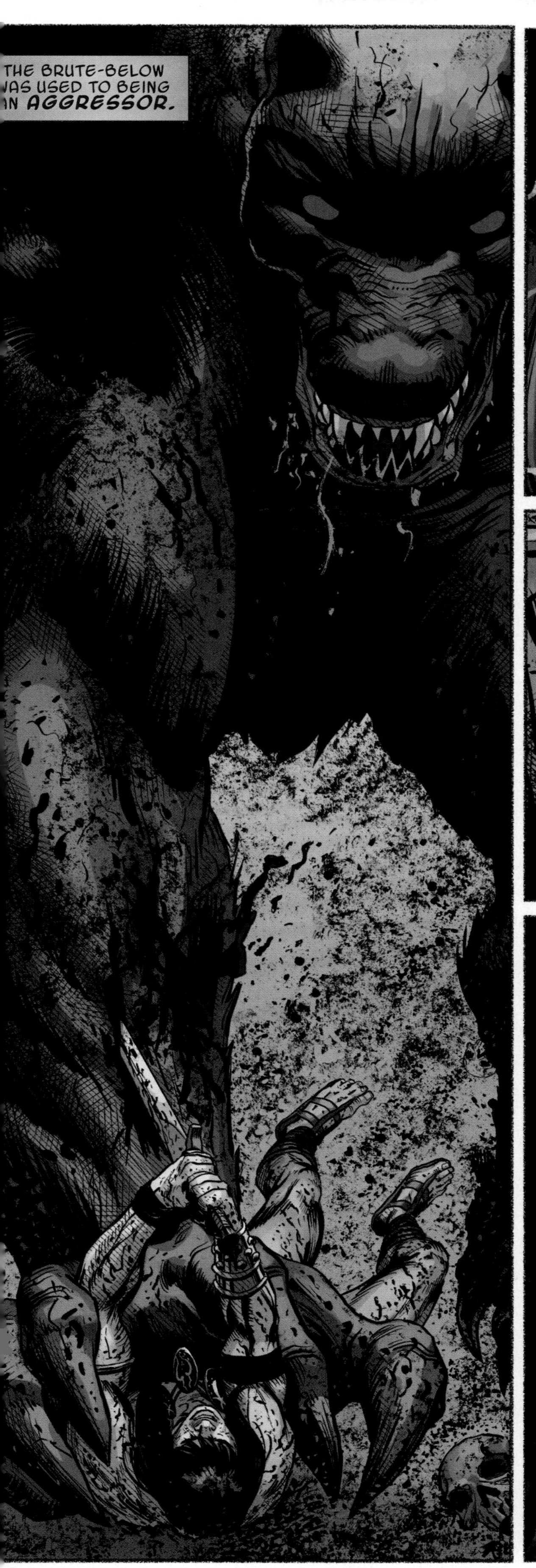
THE BRUTE-BELOW WAS USED TO BEING AN **AGGRESSOR.**

MOST OF ITS VICTIMS WOULD GO **LIMP** AS SOON AS IT STRUCK.

BUT IT HAD **NEVER** FACED A FOE LIKE THIS **CIMMERIAN...**
YARRGH!!!

...AN **INDOMITABLE WILL** TEMPERED WITH **ENDLESS RAGE.**

THE CREATURE'S FIRST INSTINCT IS TO **BATTER** THIS NUISANCE UNTIL HE STOPS MOVING...

...AND THE SOUND OF THAT **CRUSHING ASSAULT** REVERBERATES THROUGH THE DEMON'S DEN AS THE CAGED FLOOR **SHAKES** AND **SHUDDERS.**

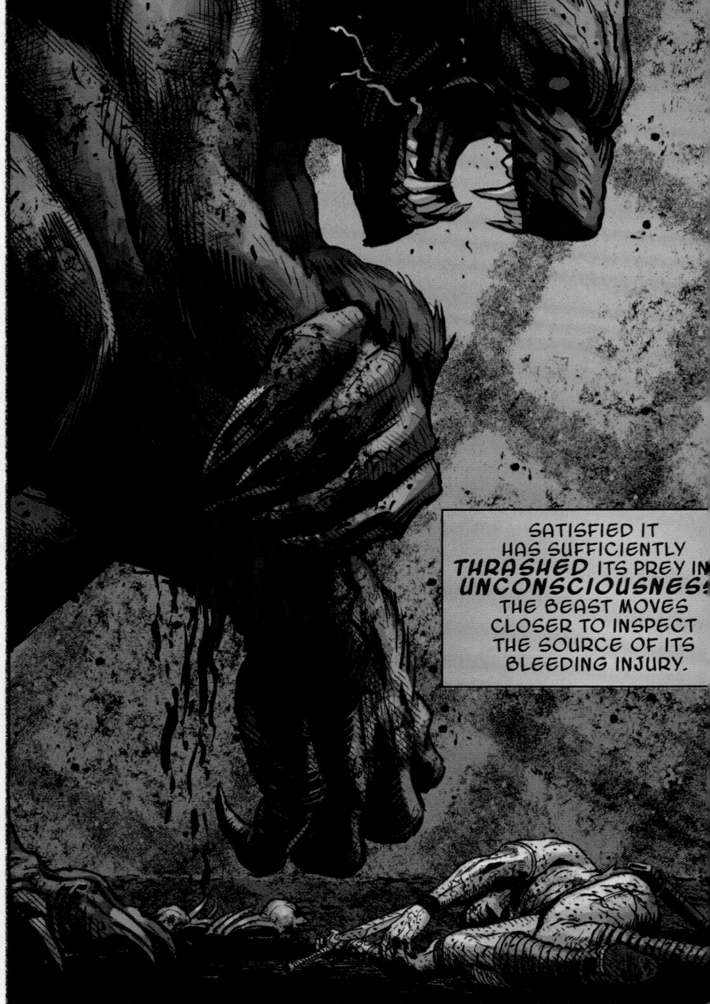
SATISFIED IT HAS SUFFICIENTLY **THRASHED** ITS PREY IN **UNCONSCIOUSNES** THE BEAST MOVES CLOSER TO INSPECT THE SOURCE OF ITS BLEEDING INJURY.

IS MEAL SMELLS LIKE THERS THE CREATURE HAS FEASTED UPON. NORMALLY IT WOULD TEAR THE BODY INTO PIECES AND FEED...

AND THERE YOU HAVE IT.
KESHAN, KOTHIAN, OR CIMMERIAN... IT DOESN'T MATTER.
THEY'RE ALL JUST MORSELS FOR THE BRUTE.

...AND YET, THIS TIME, IT HESITATES.

PERHAPS THE CREATURE SENSES ITS FATE.

THIS MEAT WILL NOT LIE STILL...

...THIS WARRIOR WILL NOT YIELD...

...AND DEATH WILL BE DELIVERE
UPON A SLIVER OF STEEL...

THE CROWD IS AWED INTO SILENCE BY THIS KILLING STRIKE.
NOT A SOUND IS MADE UNTIL CONAN'S VOICE ECHOES FROM BELOW.
PRAY NOW TO YOUR FUTILE GODS, YOU WRETCHES...
...BECAUSE THIS CIMMERIAN WILL HAVE HIS REVENGE.
AND THEN, UNEXPECTEDLY, EVERY TORCH IN THE DEMON'S DEN IS SUDDENLY SNUFFED OUT...
...WHILE THE GODSEND GEMSTONE SHIMMERS WITH AN ENCHANTING GLOW LIKE NO OTHER.

THE WARM ILLUMINATION OF THE EMERALD THAT ONCE SOOTHED IS NOW A SEARING AND STROBING FUROR THAT WILL NOT BE DENIED.

WHEREVER ITS LIGHT TOUCHES...

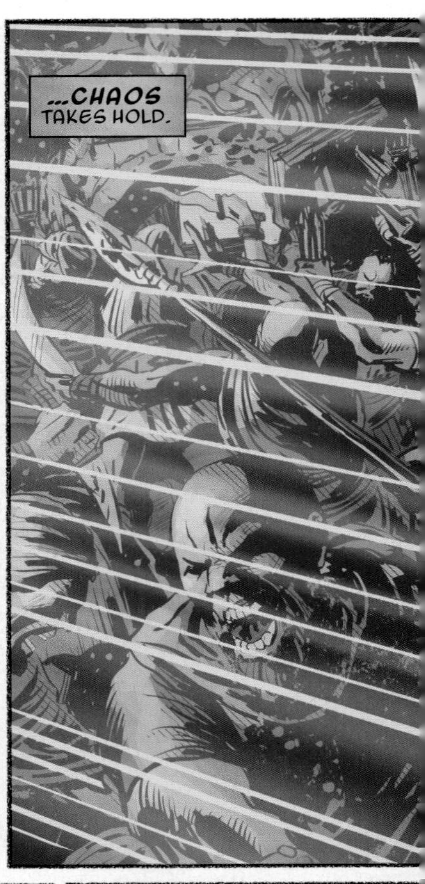
...CHAOS TAKES HOLD.

WHAT MADNESS IS THIS?!

WHATEVER CAUSED IT, I'LL TAKE THE BOON AND USE ITS DISTRACTION TO BREAK FREE!

TIME SPUTTERS AND SPINS--
--IN BURSTS OF BLOODSHED FRAMED IN FLASHES OF GREEN.
SOUNDS ECHO AND RIPPLE WITH WAVES OF VIOLENCE AS METAL CLASHES WITH SCREAMS.

A SAVAGE CASCADE...
THE GEM'S LIGHT OBEYED...

LIGHT, LIGHT!

WHERE'S THE DAMN LIGHT?!

WHAT WAS IT YOU SAID?
"THE DEN WILL HAVE ITS DUE."
FAIR ENOUGH, WORM...
...I'VE COME TO COLLECT.

THIS TRULY IS A DEMON'S DEN...
N'UH!

...A FOUL PIT OF DISGRACEFUL DEGENERATES PLAYING WITH LIVES AS THEY FESTER IN THEIR SELFISH WEALTH.
G'UAAAH!

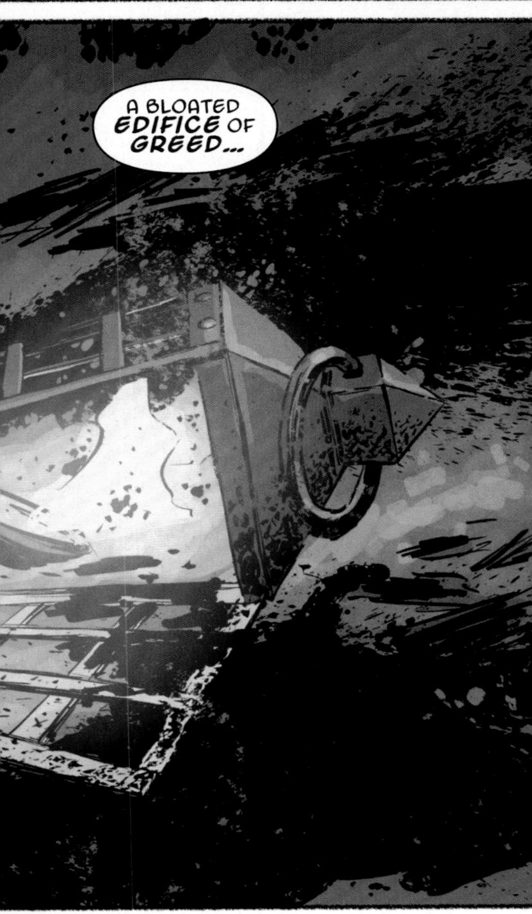
A BLOATED EDIFICE OF GREED...

...NOW JUST A CORPSE FIT TO BE BURNED.

AND BURN IT DOES.
THE HUNGRY FIRE CATCHES QUICKLY UPON THE DRY WOOD AND DUSTY AIR.
THICK PLUMES OF BLACK SMOKE AND ASH SOON SPOUT UP TO THE CEILING.
THE CONFLAGRATION TAKES HOLD WITH SUCH EASE THAT CONAN WONDERS IF SOME UNSEEN FORCE ENCOURAGES ITS INTENSITY.
BEFORE THE HEAT AND SMOKE CAN OVERTAKE THE BARBARIAN, HE PUSHE PAST THE STING IN HIS LUNGS AND PAIN IN HIS LIMBS TO ESCAPE THE BLAZE...
...AND EMERGE ONCE MORE IN THE DARKENED ALLEYS OF SHADIZAR THE WICKED.

=KAFF KAFF=
=KAFF KAFF=

=KAFF KAFF=
YOU ARE QUITE THE SURVIVOR, CIMMERIAN...
...QUITE THE SURVIVOR INDEED.

YOU...
...YOU DID THIS.

OF COURSE I DID!
DID YOU TRULY THINK SUCH SPLENDOR AND STRIFE OCCURRED ON THEIR OWN?

ALL IS AS I HAVE WILLED IT.
"THE MOMENT I SENSED YOUR ARRIVAL IN SHADIZAR, I PUT ASSASSINS UPON MARAUDUS AND HIS MEN, ENSURING YOU WOULD FIND HIM IN HIS MOMENT OF DESPERATE NEED.
"WHEN I SAW YOUR STRENGTH UP CLOSE, I KNEW YOU WERE THE RIGHT CHOICE...
"...AND SO, THE TRAP WAS SET...
"...SPRUNG...
"...AND YOU WERE SET UPON THE PATH I REQUIRED.
5
4
"THE PERFECT PAWN IN A GAME WORTHY OF A GOD."

CROM'S BLOOD, WOMAN!
YOU TRICKED ME AND TURNED HAT HALL INTO A LAUGHTERHOUSE OF FIRE AND DEATH... FOR WHAT?!

FOR THIS, OF COURSE.
YOU WERE A MARVELOUS DISTRACTION, PROVIDING COVER SO I COULD TAKE THE GODSEND AND PUNISH THOSE WHO ABUSED ITS GLORY.

SO YOU'RE A WITCH AND A THIEF?

A "THIEF"?
I THINK NOT.
YOU SEE ONLY WHAT YOU WANT TO SEE, MY SIMPLE BARBARIAN.

ONE CANNOT STEAL ONE'S OWN SELF.

AS THE MYSTERIOUS EMERALD SHATTERS, A SWIRLING VORTEX OF COSMIC ENERGY IS UNLEASHED...
...AND KYALA, GODDESS OF LUCK AND DESTINY, REGAINS THE MISSING PIECE OF HER DEIFIC MIGHT.
CONAN IS BLINDED BY THIS AWE-INSPIRING DISPLAY OF CELESTIAL POWER.
HIS PRIMAL SCREAM IS SWALLOWED BY THE RAGING STORM OF HER MAJESTY.
AS THE CIMMERIAN FALLS BACK TO HIS KNEES AND HIS SENSES SLOWLY RETURN...
...HE HEARS THE FADING WORDS OF MOTHER FATE...
"TONIGHT A PAWN, BUT NOT FOREVER..."

CONAN THE GAMBLER
PART 3
LUCK IS A LADY
End

10 ◇ DARK CAVERN, DARK CRYSTAL PART ONE

"Know, oh prince, that between the years when the oceans drank Atlantis and the gleaming cities, and the years of the rise of the Sons of Aryas, there was an age undreamed of, when shining kingdoms lay spread across the world like blue mantles beneath the stars...Hither came Conan, the Cimmerian, black-haired, sullen-eyed, sword in hand, a thief, a reaver, a slayer, with gigantic melancholies and gigantic mirth, to tread the jeweled thrones of the Earth under his sandaled feet."

--The Nemedian Chronicles

DARK CAVERN
DARK CRYSTAL
HHGNNN...
RRRRGGG
THE TWO TOWERING FLESH-CARVED FIGURES ARE A WORLD--A COSMOS UNTO THEMSELVES.
THEIR EYES ARE RIVETED ON NOTHING BUT EACH OTHER...
THEY HEAR NO SOUNDS SAVE THEIR OWN DEEP-THROATED GRUNTS AND PANTING BREATHS...

...YET OTHER NOISES SWIRL ABOUT THEM, HAD THEY BUT THE WILL AND WHIM TO HEED THEM...
THIRTY ORICHS ON THE BIG AFGHULI!
BET TAKEN, ARGOSSEAN! DID I TELL YOU TO STOP POURING, WENCH?
MY SIX TAMRAS SAY THE WESTERN DOG TAKES HIM IN THE END!

THE MAN'S GOT THE N BULK—BUT I'LL R TEN MANNATS THE BRONZED BARBARIAN!
'LL R THAT TH GOOD OHYAN WARS!
HOW ABOUT IT, OLD MAN? THIS FISTFUL OF ZINJAS ON THE NORTHMAN!
NOT SO FAST! I'LL SEE WHICH ONE GETS BLOODED FIRST BEFORE I SHOW THE COLOR OF MY MONEY.
MY MONTH'S WAGES ARE RIDING ON THE AFGHULI.
I SURE HOPE YOU WIN, SWEETNESS!
CUT HIM, HILLMAN! CUT HIM IN TWO!
MAKE IT SEVEN! I FANCY THAT GOLD EARRING YOU'RE SPORTING!

NNNHH...
HRRRR...

HAH!
DAMN!

ALL RIGHT, YOU WHINING ZINGARAN RAT! I'M IN!
MY PILE--AGAINST YOURS!
NOT FAIR, PATCH! MY MAN TRIPPED!

STILL, IN FOR A ZINJA--
--IN FOR A POUND OF FLESH!
HNNNNGH!

OOOPH

YOU ERE... OLDING ACK!
FOR THAT, I'LL HAVE YOUR GUTS FOR MY SCABBARD!
COME AND TAKE THEM!
RGGG!
URKK!
FIGHT'S OVER.
I'M SURE HE'S TELLING ASURA HE'S SORRY HE STARTED IT.

THE OUTSIDER MADE IT LOOK... SO EASY...
NEVER MIND THAT. PAY UP!
THAT'S MY GIRL!
MY COINS AND HIS-- AND NOW THEY'RE ALL...

...MINE.

ALL RIGHT... SO A FEW OF THEM ARE MINE, ANYWAY.
ONE.
TWO, SURELY...
ONE.
YES, THAT'S WHAT I SAID. ONE.

AFTER THE AFGHULI CHALLENGED ME, YOU TOOK LONG ENOUGH TO GET THE STAKES HIGH ENOUGH, SIMINO.
WITH ALL DUE RESPECT, CIMMERIAN, IT WAS YOUR FAULT.
WHEN THEY SAW THOSE SINEWS, IT

STILL, ANY TIME YOU WANT TO TEAM UP FOR A BIT MORE FUN AND GAMING...
I'LL GIVE A SHOUT DOWN YOUR RATHOLE.
THAT WAS EXPERTLY DONE, OUTLANDER...

...MOST EXPERTLY, INDEED!
I'VE SEEN BETTER, MILADY.
WELL, I HAVE NOT.
DO I KNOW YOU TWO?
I KNOW OF YOU, PERHAPS... IF YOUR NAME IS GUPTAR.
SORRY.
THAT'S GUPTAR.
PITY. I WAS ADVISED TO HIRE HIM AS A GUARD FOR MY LITTLE EXPEDITION.
TOO BAD YOU DIDN'T ASK HIM YESTERDAY.
PERHAPS YES...PERHAPS NO. AFTER ALL, YOU KILLED HIM.
DESPITE YOUR RECENT WINDFALL, IS THERE A CHANCE YOU MIGHT ACCOMPANY US INTO THE HIMELIAN MOUNTAINS?
IF YOU'VE MONEY TO PAY WITH...NOT JUST WINSOME LOOKS.
HERE, LASS. BUY YOURSELF A SKIRT WITHOUT A TEAR IN IT.
I'VE BEEN AT LOOSE ENDS IN THIS PLACE WITH ONE FOOT IN VENDHYA, THE OTHER IN AFGHULISTAN.

I AM SERRA...AND I'VE COME ALL THE WAY FROM CORINTHIA.
TRULY, I'VE HAD THE LUCK OF THE GODS TO FIND FIRST ZUBAIR BACK IN AYODHYA--AND NOW YOU--TO HELP ME IN MY QUEST.
LUCK, YES.
I'M LESS SURE ABOUT THE "GODS" PART.
OH, AND I'M CONAN, A CIMMERIAN.
WE DON'T NEE THIS UNCOU SAVAGE, LA SERRA.
YOU'VE SEEN MY SWORDWORK-- SO YOU KNOW YOU NEED NO MORE TO KEEP YOU SAFE.

WHAT I NEED IS MY DECISION, ZUBAIR-- SINCE I'M THE ONE PAYING BOTH YOUR WAGES.
AND I'D HIRE FIFTY BLADES TO ACCOMPANY ME IF I COULD--BUT I'M ONLY A POOR NOBLEWOMAN.

AS YOU WISH, MILADY.
I MEANT NO OFFENSE, NORTHRON.

NONE TAKEN...FOR NOW.
AS ZUBAIR KNOWS, MY BROTHER, LORD FALLO, LED A PARTY INTO THE HIMELIANS.
HE HAD COME INTO A MAP POINTING TO A GREAT TREASURE HIDDEN WITHIN ONE OF THE PEAKS...

...BUT HE-- HE NEVER RETURNED!
I'VE PLEDGED MY LANDS--EVEN MY TITLE--TO LORDS BACK HOME TO RAISE THE COST OF THIS EXPEDITION.
ALIVE OR-- OR DEAD--I'M DETERMINED TO FIND HIM...!
NOR, I ASSUME, WILL YOU MIND ACQUIRING THE TREASURE...IF IT'S THERE FOR THE FINDING.
NO MATTER. I'LL SELL YOU MY SWORD FOR A TIME.

EXCELLENT! WE'LL LEAVE ON THE MORROW.
NOW COME. WE MUST FINISH SECURING SUPPLIES FOR THE TRIP.

AFTER YOU, BARBARIAN.
IF IT'S ALL THE SAME WITH YOU, VENDHYAN...
...I WOULD PREFER TO BE THE ONE WITH NO ONE AT HIS BACK.

OH... THERE YOU ARE.
I FEARED I'D LOST YOU BOTH.

DAWN IS BUT A HALF-WHISPERED SUGGESTION WHEN THE TINY EXPEDITION BEGINS ITS LONG, ARDUOUS SLOG.
NEITHER BREATH NOR WORD IS WASTED, FOR THE ASCENT IS GRADUAL BUT RELENTLESS--AND THESE ARE STILL BUT THE FOOTHILLS OF THE TOWERING HIMELIANS.
BY MIDDAY, THE BORDER TOWN IS LOST IN MISTY DISTANCE BEHIND THEM...THE CLOUD-MAULING MOUNTAINS NEARLY AS FAR-OFF AS EVER.

WITH THE FALL OF NIGHT, THE ENTOURAGE HALTS IN THE STONE SHADOW OF WHAT ALL PRESENT KNOW WILL BE AN EVEN STEEPER CLIMB, COME MORNING...
MAYBE ZUBAIR IS HAPPY TO FOLLOW YOU TO THE HIGH ENDS OF THE EARTH, WOMAN...
..BUT IF I'M TO RISK MY E GUARDING RS, I'D LIKE A MPSE OF YOUR OPY OF YOUR ROTHER'S MAP...
...OR AT LEAST HEAR WHAT YOU CAN TELL US ABOUT THE TREASURE HE HOPED TO FIND.
NOT AN UNREASONABLE REQUEST, CIMMERIAN.

AD A COPY OF THE , YES...BUT I DARED OT RISK IT BEING TAKEN FROM ME...
SO I BURNED IT... AFTER I HAD MEMORIZED IT, OF COURSE...

THAT'S NOT HALF SO SMART AS YOU SUPPOSE.
THAT MERELY ASSURES A RIVAL WOULD TORTURE YOU TO MAKE YOU LEAD HIM TO THE HIDDEN HOARD.

I...
I GUESS I NEVER THOUGHT OF THAT.

AFTER THE SHAKEN CORINTHIAN RETIRES TO HER CRUDE TENT, CONAN WATCHES ZUBAIR DRIFT TO THE EDGE OF THE CAMP.
HE GIVES HIS GRIM CO-TRAVELER A FEW MOMENTS ALONE WITH HIS THOUGHTS...BEFORE HE DRAWS NEAR...
WHAT DO YOU MAKE OF THE LADY'S TREASURE TALE, VENDHYAN?
I DO NOT KNOW WHAT YOU KNOW OF THE WAYS OF THIS ANCIENT EASTERN KINGDOM, BARBARIAN.
BUT I WAS THE SECOND SON OF A LORD OF AYODHYA...AND SECOND SONS INHERIT ONLY WHAT THE FIRST SON HAS NO USE FOR.
SO I MUST MAKE MY WAY IN THE WORLD BY MY SWORD NOW.
FORTUNATELY, I HAVE NEVER MET MY EQUAL WITH A BLADE...
...AND THE LADY SERRA SAW ENOUGH OF MY SKILL TO KNOW I COULD SLICE MY WAY THROUGH A HUNDRED MEN ON HER BEHALF.

I'VE BEEN A SELLSWORD MYSELF SINCE MY YOUNGER DAYS, ZUBAIR.
IT WAS MY SECOND VOCATION.
OH? AND DARE I ASK WHAT WAS THE FIRST?

I WAS A THIEF.

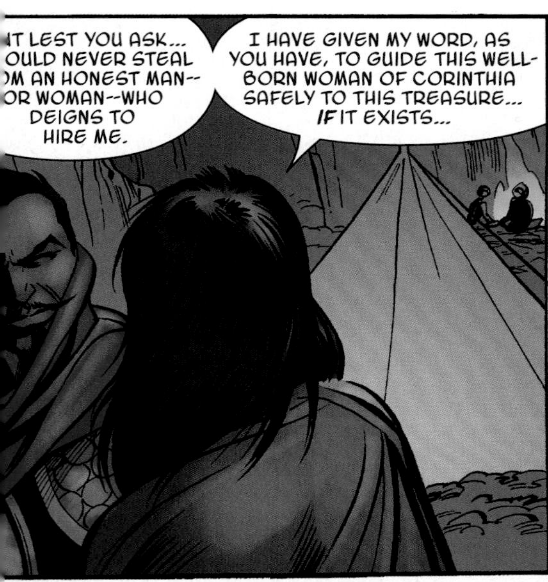

IT LEST YOU ASK... OULD NEVER STEAL OM AN HONEST MAN-- OR WOMAN--WHO DEIGNS TO HIRE ME.
I HAVE GIVEN MY WORD, AS YOU HAVE, TO GUIDE THIS WELL-BORN WOMAN OF CORINTHIA SAFELY TO THIS TREASURE... *IF* IT EXISTS...

...EVEN THOUGH I'VE AN ERRAND OF MY *OWN* TO TEND TO ALONG THE WAY.

THE DAY DAWNS.
THEN ANOTHER.
AND, JUST ABOUT THE TIME MOST OF THE CLIMBERS WOULD HAVE TO PROD THEIR MEMORIES TO RECALL PRECISELY HOW MANY DAYS THEY HAVE BEEN TRUDGING UP THE GRADUALLY STEEPER AND ROCKIER SLOPES...

...THAT SUDDENLY BECOMES THE *LEAST* OF THE MATTERS THAT CLUTTER THEIR MINDS.
GET BACK!
OHHH...

HO, BELOW!
I ASSUME THAT ANY WHO WOULD TRAVERSE THE TERRITORY OF THE AFGHULIS~

--ARE PREPARED TO PAY FOR THE PRIVILEGE!
HERE'S WHERE YOU EARN YOUR WAGES, YOU TWO!
DO YOU MEAN TO COLLECT YOUR ROBBER'S TRIBUTE YOURSELF, AFGHULI?
I WOULD NOT DIRTY MY HANDS.
MY HILLMEN, HOWEVER, ARE FAR LESS CHOOSY!
WHAT WOULD YOU HAVE US DO NOW, MILADY?
FOR THE MOMENT... WAIT.

YOU MUST BE PAKIM, CHIEFTAIN OF THE AFGHULIS.
HAH! DID YOU HEAR THAT, LADS?
MY FAME IS SPREADING BY THE DAY!

IT HAS NOT SPREAD THAT FAR, YOU GRIZZLED ROGUE. ONLY TO SILVAGARH.
ALL THE SAME, YOU ARE THE REASON I AM HERE.

WHAT? DID YOU ACCOMPANY ME--ONLY SO YOU COULD DESERT ME AND JOIN THESE BRIGANDS?
I WILL HONOR MY OBLIGATIONS TO YOU.
BUT I WILL ADMIT THAT I HAD THIS...OTHER THING IN MIND, AS WELL.

EAR ME, LLMEN!
I AM CONAN...FROM CIMMERIA, A NORTHERN LAND WHOSE HILLS ARE EVEN ROCKIER AND ROUGHER THAN THESE.
I HAVE COMMANDED THE ARMY OF DESERT-GIRDED KHORAJA--CAPTAINED PIRATES ON THE VILAYET SEA--AND BEEN HETMAN OF THE FIERCE KOZAKS WHO HARRIED TURAN.
SO WHY ARE YOU HERE--AT THE TIMBERLINE OF THE HIMELIAN FOOTHILLS?

ECAUSE I AM THE N WHO CAN WELD YOU DOGS--
NTO THE GHTING RCE YOU RE BORN TO BE!
STILL YOUR TONGUE, JACKAL!

PAKIM IS HETMAN OF THE AFGHULIS!
AND HAS BEEN--FOR THE PAST TWO YEARS, SAY THE RUMORS THAT DRIFT DOWN TO THE BORDER TOWN.

AND WHAT HAVE YOU DONE IN THAT TIME TO FULFILL THE DREAM OF EVERY INHABITANT OF THESE HILLS WORTH HIS SALT?
WHAT HAVE YOU DONE TO END VENDHYA'S CLAIMS TO THESE UNTAMED LANDS--
--AND TURN THE AFGHULIS INTO WHAT THEY KNOW THEY ARE DESTINED TO BE--
--THE GREATEST POWER BETWEEN VENDHYA AND TURAN?!

YOU OUTLAND PIG!
DID YOU EXPECT ME TO JUST STAND ASIDE AND LET YOU TAKE MY PLACE?

NO, PAKIM.
I EXPECT YOU TO FIGHT ME--
--AND I EXPECT TO KILL YOU.

BUT A TRUE CHIEFTAIN DOES NOT LOWER HIMSELF TO CROSS SWORDS WITH EVERY

THE HILL CODE IS WELL-KNOWN FAR AND WIDE.
IT SAYS A HETMAN MUST FIGHT ANY MAN WHO CHALLENGES HIM BEFORE THE ASSEMBLED TRIBE.
WELL, PAKIM? WHAT DO YOU SAY?
I SAY--

NOW!

WE HEAR AND OBEY, GREAT PAKIM!
CROM'S DEVILS!

GOOD WORK, DHUUL!
NNNFF!
I KNEW IT WAS WISE TO KEEP YOU FEW IN HIDING WITH A NET!

CAN YOU DO NOTHING, ZUBAIR?
I COULD BEST THEM ALL, ONE BY ONE-- EVEN BY TWOS OR THREES--BUT NOT THE LOT OF THEM.

YOU ARE A HIND-LICKING DOG TO VIOLATE THE HILL CODE!
HE SPEAKS TRUE, PAKIM! YOU SHOULD NOT HAVE--
SILENCE-- OR I'LL DO TO YOU WHAT I MEAN TO DO TO THIS OFFAL!

OUR CODE, PAKIM!
YOU MUST ABIDE BY THE CODE!
I--
THE BARBARIAN, MY CHIEFTAIN--HE STRIVES TO ESCAPE!
STOP HIM!
DOG! IT WAS YOUR MAN WHO PULLED ME OFF MY FEET--
--BUT BY ALL THE GODS OF VENDHYA AND LANDS WEST--
--I'LL CUT MY WAY TO YOU--
--AND INTO YOU!

I HAVE HIM!
KRAK
AARRRGG!

SHALL I GUT HIM, PAKIM, BEFORE HE REGAINS HIS SENSES?
BY ASURA, DHUUL--YOU ARE A READER OF MY THOUGHTS!

HIS IS
T RIGHT,
PAKIM!
THE CODE OF OUR FATHERS' FATHERS--
YES--YOU ARE RIGHT! PAKIM WILL HONOR THE CODE.
THAT IS GOOD! NOW, LET US--

DOG OF A DOG!
SLSSH
AAAAAA!
HE STABBED HELAI!

YE--AND SO DHUUL AND HIS
HORTS AND I WILL TREAT ANY
MAN WHO RAILS AGAINST MY ORDERS!
FOOLS! THINK YOU THIS HIGHBORN WESTERN FEMALE CAME HERE FOR THE VIEW FROM THE MOUNTAINTOP?
I SPIED ON HER AND HER LACKEYS...

SHE CAME HERE LOOKING FOR A
EASURE--TO WHICH ONLY SHE CAN LEAD US.
I...WILL DO SO!
PLEASE-- DO NOT HARM ME!
WE'LL LET THIS CITY DWELLER LIVE LONG ENOUGH TO CARRY THE LOOT BACK FOR US.

TIE THAT SHUMARITAN, OR WHATEVER HE IS, TO YONDER TREE UNTIL I RETURN!
AND KEEP TO HIM HIS LIFE, IF YOU VALUE YOUR OWN--
--TILL I, AND I ALONE, FLAY HIM ALIVE FOR HIS INSOLENCE IN TRYING TO USURP MY RIGHTFUL PLACE!
WHO KNOWS, LADS--

--IF THIS STORIED TREASURE IS RIPE IN VARIETY AND FORMS--
--HE MIGHT BECOME THE FIRST MAN AT THIS TIMBERLINE TO HAVE HIS SKIN STRIPPED FROM HIS BONE BY A GOLDEN DAGGER!

11 ◇ DARK CAVERN, DARK CRYSTAL PART TWO

"Know, oh prince, that between the years when the oceans drank Atlantis and the gleaming cities, and the years of the rise of the Sons of Aryas, there was an age undreamed of, when shining kingdoms lay spread across the world like blue mantles beneath the stars...Hither came Conan, the Cimmerian, black-haired, sullen-eyed, sword in hand, a thief, a reaver, a slayer, with gigantic melancholies and gigantic mirth, to tread the jeweled thrones of the Earth under his sandaled feet."

--The Nemedian Chronicles

PTUI
GOT HIM, BY ASURA!

SQUARE ON THE LEFT CHEEK!
YOU MIGHT AS WELL HAND OVER OUR WAGER STAKES RIGHT NOW!
NOT SO FAST, CHUPA!

I HAVEN'T HAD MY TURN YET!
PTUII

HAH! YOUR SHOT BARELY MADE IT TO THE BARBARIAN'S CHEST!
THAT ONE WAS JUST TO GET THE RANGE! NOW--

PTUUI
THERE! RIGHT DEAD CENTER IN HIS UGLY FACE!

PAY UP!
IN YOUR MADDEST DREAM! OUR BET WAS ONE SPIT TAKES ALL, SO--

YOU HILL-BRED, HAIR-FACED JACKALS--

YOU CAN FINISH YOUR DAMNED GAME--
--NNGGN...
--IN WHATEVER HELL WILL HOLD YOU!
RRRAA
THE OUTLANDER-- HE'S FREE!
NO, HE ISN'T! HE'S JUST RIPPED OUT THE TRUNK'S ROTTED BRANCHES!
HE'S STILL BOUND! GRAB YOUR BLADE AND WE'LL GUT HIM!
DARK CAVERN, DARK CRYSTA
PART

IN YOUR EYES, I'M A MAN SHACKLED!
IN MINE-- I WIELD TWO JAGGED CLUBS!
HE'S LIKE A DEMON OUT OF NARA-YAM!
WAKE UP, DOG-BROTHERS! W-WE NEED YOUR HELP!
THOSE DRUNKEN SOTS?
THERE'S NOT ONE WHO'S FIT TO STAND, LET ALONE WIELD A KNIFE!
THEN I'LL CARVE YOU LIKE A YAK...
HOLD HIM, DESU--
HNNNH

WHOOPH
--AND I'LL CUT OUT HIS HEART AS A FEAST FOR THE BUZZARDS!

THE BUZZARDS WILL FILL THEIR BELLIES, RIGHT ENOUGH--
YYAARRR
--BUT NOT--
--ON ME!
OOOG
NEVER TIE A MAN TO A TREE AT THE HIGHEST EDGE OF THE TIMBERLINE.
I'LL HAVE TO TELL THAT TO PAKIM WHEN I SEE HIM...

Some hours' march above the hillmen's camp...
YOU'RE STALLING, WOMAN!
DO YOU THINK WE'RE GOING TO CARRY YOUR PERFUMED HIDE JUST BECAUSE YOU PRETEND TO FALL?
PLEASE-- THE SNOW! I'M-- NOT USED TO WALKING IN IT!
JUST GIVE ME--A MOMENT TO REST, AND I'LL--

DID OUR HETMAN ASK YOU TO TALK, WITCH?
JUST SHOW US TO THE TREASURE CAVE!
DON'T STRIKE TOO HARD, DHUUL!
OHHH

CARCASS ULD BE OF NO USE TO US.
ZUBAIR-- I PAID YOU TO PROTECT ME...
YOU MAY HAVE NOTICED I MYSELF AM A PRISONER, MILADY SERRA.
I CONTEND THAT RENDERS OUR CONTRACT NULL AND VOID.

HELP ME UP, PAKIM--AND I WILL SHOW YOU TO THE TREASURE.
I KNOW... WHEN I AM BEATEN.

THAT'S MORE LIKE IT! NOW WHERE--
MY KNEES BUCKLED-- WHEN I SUDDENLY REALIZED WE'RE SO NEAR THE CAVERN SHOWN ON MY BROTHER'S MAP.
THE ENTRANCE SHOULD BE--JUST AHEAD!
YET, WITH THE SNOW COVER, WE CAN SEE ONLY THE MOUNTAIN'S OWN FACE.
DON'T STRIKE ME AGAIN--I BEG YOU--
--AND I SWEAR BY MITRA I'LL FIND IT FOR YOU!
COME BACK HERE, WOMAN!

COME BAAAAAAAAAAAAAAAAAA
IS ANYONE HURT? IF SHE LED US INTO A TRAP--!
WE WERE WALKING ATOP A PATCH OF ICE--AND IT GAVE WAY!
BUT LOOK, PAKIM--
LOOK, ALL OF YOU!

THIS IS THE PLACE POOR FALLO TOLD ME ABOUT-- THE CAVERN OF THE DARK CRYSTAL!
ASURA AND DANAVA!
IF WE HAD FALLEN A FEW HANDS TO THE LEFT OR RIGHT--!
BUT WE DID NOT--A SURETY THAT THE GODS FAVOR US!
WAS THE INTERIOR MAPPED BY YOUR BROTHER--OR MUST WE STUMBLE ABOUT WITH ONLY THIS TORCH FOR OUR GUIDE?
AS I TOLD YOU, I MEMORIZED THAT MAP BEFORE I BURNED IT.
THIS WAY...I THINK.

...GODS SAVE US, WE'VE WALKED A LEAGUE, IF WE'VE WALKED AN INCH!
SHUT YOUR TEETH, YOU PANICKY FOOL!
STILL, IF YOU'RE SEEKING TO DELAY US, WOMAN--

HAVE YOU NOT HEARD IT SAID...
...THAT IT IS ALWAYS DARKEST JUST BEFORE DAWN'S FIRST BEAM?

THAT SPHERE--IT THROBS AS IF IT WERE HALF SUN, HALF BEATING HEART!
YOU CALLED IT THE "DARK CRYSTAL"-- YET SURELY ITS LIGHT COMES FROM WITHIN!

NO MATTER! MEN WILL PLEDGE THEIR SOULS AS A MERE FIRST PAYMENT FOR THIS PULSING GEM!
BUT, IS ALL ITS VALUE IN ITS RADIANCE, CORINTHIAN--OR HAS IT ALSO SOME MAGIC TO BESTOW?

PERHAPS YOU WILL HAVE YOUR ANSWERS, HILLMAN...
...IF YOU RAISE YOUR TORCH A BIT.
EH?

EEEEE
WHAT IN THE DEVILS' NAMES ARE THOSE THINGS?
EVERY TREASURE HAS ITS GUARDIANS.
THESE SLEEPING ONES ARE THE KEEPERS OF THE DARK CRYSTAL!

YOU KNEW WE'D FIND THESE THINGS HERE?
I KNEW THEY WERE HERE--AND YOU KNEW WHERE "HERE" WAS.
SO I FOUND YOU--AND MADE YOU BELIEVE YOU HAD FOUND ME.

I ALSO KNEW THERE WAS A TINY SHARD CHIPPED OFF THE SPHERE--
--WHICH CURRENTLY RESIDES IN THAT RING YOU WEAR.
WE BOTH KNOW THAT THE DARK CRYSTAL MUST BE WHOLE BEFORE IT CAN FULLY FUNCTION...

...AND IT WILL BE WHOLE--WHEN YOU FIT THAT RING SHARD INTO ITS PROPER PLACE!
BY ASURA'S EYES, YOU'VE BOTH BEEN PLAYING ME FOR A FOOL!
NO, PAKIM...

YOU ARE A FOOL!
AGNA VALU!
SORCERY-- OR I'M HANUMAN'S MONKEY!

DHUUL! CLEAVE THAT DEVIL!
AYE, HETMAN! ESCAPE ARTIST HE MAY BE--BUT HE'S HELPLESS WITHOUT HIS SWORD!
HE IS NEVER HELPLESS WHO CAN SAY--
VARUDA MARU--

--RISHYA SIPALA--
URGGG

--QIM!
SNAPT

CHREE CHREE CHREE CHREE CHREE CHREE
DO YOU HEAR THAT, YOU HAPLESS DOG OF THE HILLS?
THAT IS THE SOUND OF THE CRYSTAL'S GUARDIANS--
--AWAKENING!
I'LL RUN YOU THROUGH, TRICKSTER--
--BEFORE YOU OR THEY CAN HARM ME!
FEAR NOT, PAKIM! NO ONE IS GOING TO TOUCH YOU--

--EXCEPT ME!

YOU! THE SHUMARITAN!
THE NAME IS CONAN--OF CIMMERIA.
WHO CARES WHAT YOUR NAME IS, YOU--
A MAN SHOULD KNOW THE NAME--
--OF THE MAN--
--WHO KILLS HIM!
AAAGGKK

COME ON, WOMAN! TIME TO GO!
YOU CAME FOR ME-- AS WELL AS FOR REVENGE?
BY CROM, IS THERE SO LITTLE HONOR IN THIS WORLD THAT NO ONE BELIEVES I'D KEEP MY WORD?

OW RUN, EFORE--
NO! I CAME FOR THE CRYSTAL-- AND I CAN'T LET ZUBAIR GET IT!
YOU'VE NO CHOICE, MILADY...

YOU HAD ONLY A MAP THAT FELL BRIEFLY INTO YOUR HANDS...
...WHILE I HAVE PREPARED FOR THIS MOMENT MY ENTIRE LIFE!
VARUDA SAMURTI-- IGNA MADARA--

HREE CHREE CHREE CHREE CHREEEE
--DRATHAN!
CROM!

CHREE
CHREE
CHREEEE
CHREEEE
YYYYY
KEEP YOUR HEAD DOWN, GIRL!
THEY'RE FULLY AWAKE NOW--AND SLAYING EVERYTHING IN THIS CHAMBER!

EVERYTHING--BUT ZUBAIR!
AT PRESENT, I CAN BUT KEEP THEM AT BAY.
TO FULLY CONTROL THEM--AND THE KINGDOM THEIR CLAWS COULD CONQUER FOR ME--

--I NEED YOUR RING SHARD, LADY SERRA--
--AND I SHALL HAVE IT!

CONAN--YOU MUST RETRIEVE THE CRYSTAL FOR ME!
THE HELL I MUST!
I'M CARVING OUR WAY OUT OF HERE--IF I CAN!
ARRRR

THESE BATS FROM THE ABYSS CAN'T TOUCH ZUBAIR--
--SO, IF I CAN GET US BENEATH WHATEVER MAGIC SHIELD HE WIELDS--
CHREEEE
EEEEEKK
BY MACHA-- IF I BELIEVE ANYTHING--
--I BELIEVE THAT ANYTHING THAT LIVES--
CHREEEEEEEEEEEEEE
--CAN DIE!
YOU SLEW IT, CIMMERIAN!
BUT--WHAT'S WRONG? YOU STAGGER AS IF-- DAZED!

WHEN I STABBED THAT--THING--I SUDDENLY FELT A TERRIBLE COLD RUN UP MY BLADE AND INTO ME--
--AS IF I HAD THRUST IT INTO A CHASM OF TIME, ACROSS LOST EONS!
CROM, I HATE MAGIC!
THIS IS NO TIME FOR YOUR PERSONAL PHILOSOPHY.
MORE OF THEM--COMING AFTER US!

HOW DID ZUBAIR GET SO FAR AHEAD OF US?
HE'S ONLY WALKING--YET HE IS NEARLY OUT OF THE CAVERN!

THE BAT-DEMONS WILL CATCH US!
THEY ALREADY WOULD HAVE--BUT SOMETHING HOLDS THEM BACK!

IT CAN ONLY BE--ZUBAIR HIMSELF!
I HAD HOPED TO LE YOU REAC ME--SO I COULD GAIN THE LADY'S RING--

BUT NOW I REALIZE THAT, IF I AM TO SURVIVE THIS DAY--
--I MUST RECITE THE LONG-REMEMBERED SPELLS EVEN WITH AN INCOMPLETE CRYSTAL--
--AND TRADE THE DREAMS OF A LIFETIME--FOR A LIFE TO LIVE OUT!
ASVATI USHTA VITRI--

~DITYAS KEYA VADEVA~
HIS SPELL IS COLLAPSING THE CAVERN UPON US!
~HARVAS LAMDHARA~
--SIMHAAAAAAAAAAAA
YOU RISKED THROWING YOUR SWORD--INSTEAD OF WAITING TILL YOU COULD STAB HIM?
HOW COULD I KNOW HOW MUCH LONGER THAT DAMN SPELL OF HIS WOULD BE?
FOR ALL I KNOW, ONE MORE SYLLABLE AND WE'D BOTH BE DOWN THERE NOW, PUSHING UP ROCKS.

ONLY NOW--
THERE'S NOTHING TO KEEP THE BATS OUT OF OUR HAIR!
MAYBE WE CAN STOP THEM--WITH THE CRYSTAL!
YES! BY GODS, WOMAN--YOU'RE RIGHT!

THE CRYSTAL~

~WILL STOP THEM!
NO! DON'T THROW IT AWAY!
DID YOU WANT TO DIE?

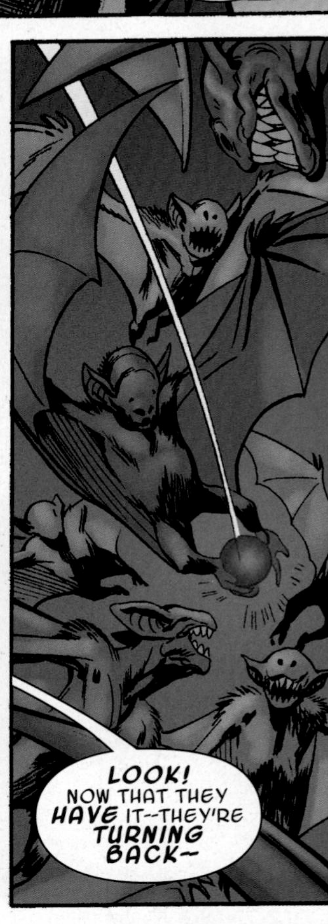
LOOK! NOW THAT THEY HAVE IT--THEY'RE TURNING BACK~

~LOSING ALL INTERES
IN US!

YOU IGNORANT BARBARIAN!
YOU COST ME THE DARK CRYSTAL!
UNNNH

YOU'D KILL ME--JUST AS YOU DOUBTLESS DID YOUR BROTHER?!
I DIDN'T POISON HIS ALE ONLY TO LOSE THE CRYSTAL TO WINGED DEVILS!
YOU--WILL REGRET STABBING ME.
WHY? DO YOU THINK YOU HAVE STRENGTH ENOUGH LEFT TO REACH ME?
IN TRUTH-- I KNOW I CAN'T--
--SO I CAN'T SAVE YOU FROM THE BAT-THING--
CHRREEEEEEEE
NNOOOOOOOOo
--THAT WAS DETERMINED TO RECLAIM THE MISSING PIECE OF THEIR DARK CRYSTAL!

AND THEN, FROM FAR BELOW-- AND FAR BEYOND--
--THERE COMES A RISING RUMBLING SOUND--LIKE THE TREAD OF UNCOUNTED STAMPEDING MASTODONS--
--AS THE CAVERN BENEATH COLLAPSES IN UPON ITSELF--
--AS IF, WITH THE DARK CRYSTAL MADE WHOLE AGAIN AT LAST-- IT AND ITS DREAD GUARDIANS WISH TO SHUT OUT THE WORLD OF MEN--
--FOR ALL TIME
THE SON OF CIMMERIA FEELS HIS SIDE.
NOT MUCH MORE THAN A FLESH WOUND, REALLY--THE LAST, INEFFECTUAL THRUST OF ONE WHO HAD RISKED ALL FOR UNTOLD WEALTH AND POWER--
--BUT WHO, IN THE END, WAS TOO WEAK OF BODY AND WILL TO CONTROL THE FORCES SHE HAD HELPED UNLEASH.
AND SO, THOUGH PERHAPS HE LIMPS JUST A LITTLE, CONAN BEGINS THE LONG, COLD TREK BACK DOWN THE MOUNTAIN.
THE HILLMEN THERE WILL SOON LEARN THEY HAVE LOST ONE HETMAN--
--AND GAINED ANOTHER, WHO WILL WELD THEM INTO A FIGHTING FORCE TO BE RECKONED WITH, THE LENGTH AND BREADTH OF ANCIENT VENDHYA.
End

#6 VARIANT
BY **MAX FIUMARA** & **MATTHEW WILSON**

#7 VARIANT
BY **PHILIP TAN** & **ANDRES MOSSA**

#8 VARIANT
BY **LEONARDO MANCO** & **RAIN BEREDO**

#9 VARIANT
BY **YASMINE PUTRI**

#10 VARIANT
BY **JOHN McCREA & MIKE SPICER**

#11 VARIANT
BY **JUAN FERREYRA**

#11 PENCILS VARIANT
BY **JUAN FERREYRA**